Essential Crochet

30 irresistible projects for you and your home

ERIKA KNIGHT

Photography by Graham Atkins Hughes

Quadrille

Editorial Director Jane O'Shea
Creative Director Helen Lewis
Project Editor Lisa Pendreigh
Editorial Assistant Laura Herring
Pattern Checker Pauline Turner
Designer Ros Holder
Photographer Graham Atkins Hughes
Stylist Jane Campsie
Hand model Gillian Herring
Production Director Vincent Smith
Production Controller Rebecca Short

This paperback edition first published in 2006 by
Quadrille Publishing Limited
Alhambra House
27–31 Charing Cross Road
London WC2H 0LS

Reprinted in 2006, 2008
10 9 8 7 6 5 4 3

Text and project designs
© 2005 Erika Knight
Photography, design and layout
© 2005 Quadrille Publishing Limited

British Library Cataloguing-in-Publication Data
A catalogue record for this book is available from
the British Library.

ISBN-13: 978 184400 308 2
ISBN-10: 1 84400 308 6

Printed in China

dedication

For all stitch makers passionate for their crafts.

Contents

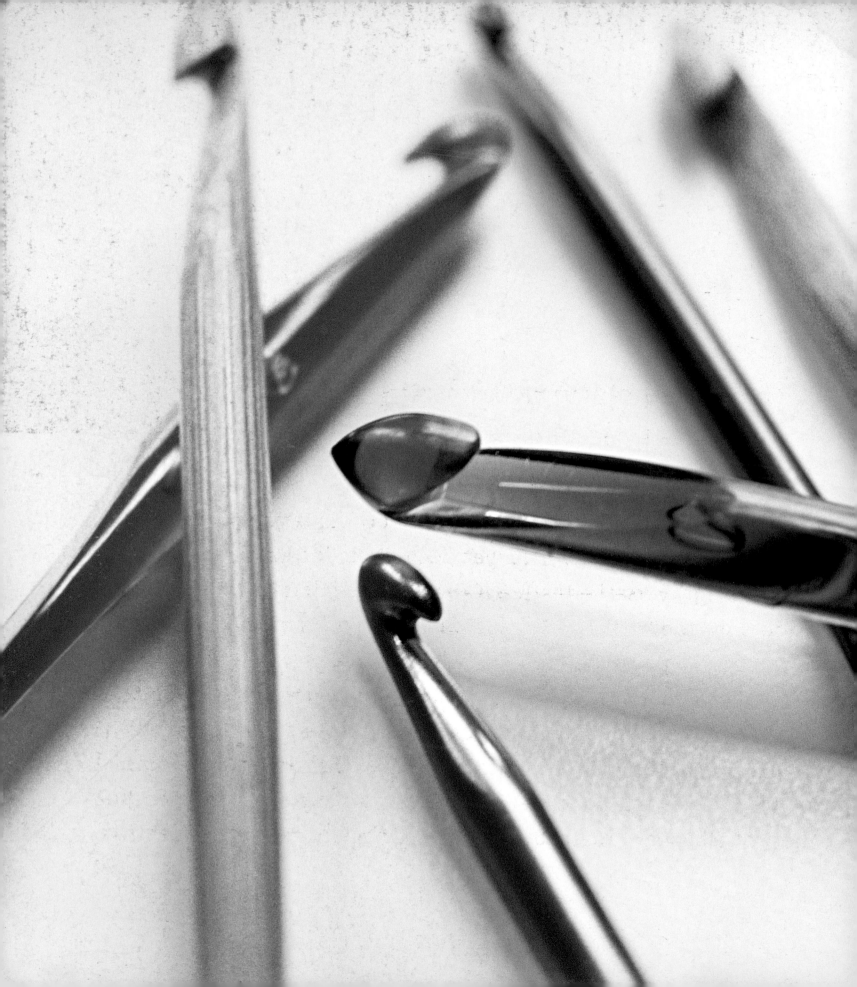

How to crochet

There is no simpler form of craft than crochet. Basic yet intricate, delicate yet durable, practical yet decorative, it creates a fabric with an amazingly versatile texture. Crochet is easy because it requires using only one hook and ball of yarn, and you can take it with you anywhere. With only a little practice, you will pick up the techniques quickly and easily and find your fingers working to a rhythm. This book concentrates on a few basic stitches, with which you will be able to make all the projects. I have designed everything in this book to bring crochet up-to-date and make it accessible. But most of all, I want to encourage you to develop your own creativity.

Yarns and texture

You can crochet with a wonderful range of yarns to produce excitingly varied textiles. The yarn and stitches you choose determine the character of the crocheted fabric, which itself is determined by the form and function of the textile. For example, a throw requires a robust yarn that will withstand plenty of wear.

You can use the texture of crochet in many ways, often with dramatic results. Some of the projects in this book have been made from unusual materials, such as leather, wire and string. Some have a tight, dense and firm structure, while others are more open and flexible.

Crochet can be worked either in rows or in the round, and squares or strips of crochet can be joined together to make patchwork or throws. The samples pictured here show the variations in texture and form that can be achieved using a variety of different threads and yarns, ranging from an aran-weight wool and a 4-ply mohair to leather and metallic wire.

Starting to crochet

To crochet easily and successfully, you need to hold the yarn and the hook comfortably, with enough tension on the yarn, so that when you draw the hook around the yarn, it stays firmly in the lip of the hook. Most people choose to wrap the yarn around their fingers, and some make an additional wrap around their little finger – choose whichever yarn-holding method works best for you. Similarly, hold the hook in whichever way you find most comfortable. Some people favour a pencil grip, while others hold the hook between their thumb and forefinger like a knife. You may even prefer to change your grip, depending on the type of stitch you are working at the time or on the size of the hook.

Wrap the ball end of the yarn around the little finger of your left hand, over the fourth, third and fore- fingers, behind the second and over the forefinger to be held in position between the forefinger and thumb. When you are starting to crochet, leave a long, loose tail end of yarn on the palm side of your hand so that you can weave this end of the yarn in on the wrong side of the finished project. Hold the hook in your right hand like a pencil.

Making the first loop

To start to crochet, you first need to make a slip loop. There are many different ways you can do this, but the method shown below is very easy to follow. You can, of course, devise your own system if you prefer.

one Make a loop in the tail end of the yarn as shown, crossing the tail end of the yarn over the ball end.

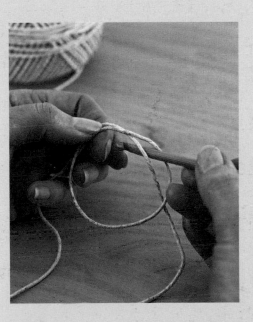

two Let the tail end drop down behind the loop, then pass the crochet hook over the loop on the right, catch the tail end with the hook and pull it through the loop.

three Holding the tail end and the ball end of the yarn in your left hand, pull the hook in the opposite direction to create the first loop on the hook. There will be a tight knot under it.

Making a foundation chain

After you have made the slip loop on your hook, the next step is to create the foundation chain for the crochet fabric. The project instructions will tell you how many chain stitches to make to start. Chain stitches are also used at the beginning of a row or round and for lace patterns.

one With the slip loop on the hook, grip the tail end of the yarn between the thumb and forefinger of your left hand.

two Hold the working yarn taut in your left hand, pass the tip of the hook in front of the yarn, then under and around it. Catch the yarn in the lip of the hook, then draw it through the loop on the hook. This completes the first chain and leaves you with one loop still on the hook.

three To make the next chain, pull a new loop through the loop on the hook. Make the number of chains required, keeping the stitches slightly loose as you will be working into them on your first row.

Slip stitch

A slip stitch is also known as 'single crochet'. If you work it into the foundation chain and continue making row after row of it, it forms a very dense, unyielding fabric. It is more commonly used to join the end and beginning of a round, or to work invisibly along the top of other stitches until you reach the required position.

one Make a foundation chain (see previous page) of the required number of chains. Insert the tip of the hook through the second chain from the hook. Catch the yarn with the hook (called 'wrap the yarn around the hook') and draw it through both the chain and the loop on the hook. This completes the first slip stitch and leaves one loop on the hook. Work the next slip stitch into the next chain in the same way. Continue as required.

Double crochet

Double crochet is sometimes also known as 'plain stitch'. It creates a dense yet flexible fabric, which is ideal for hardwearing, strong textiles. The easiest of all crochet fabrics to make, it is used frequently in this book in an exciting range of yarns, including soft wool cotton and leather. Double crochet and chain stitches can be combined to form other, softer fabrics.

one Make a foundation chain to the length you require. To make the first double crochet stitch, insert the hook through the second chain from the hook (see step 1 of slip stitch on page 13). Wrap the yarn around the hook, as shown.

two Pull the yarn through the chain as shown. There are now two loops on the hook.

three Wrap the yarn around the hook and pull the yarn through both loops. This completes the stitch.

four To make the next double crochet stitch, insert the hook through the next chain, draw a loop through, then draw the yarn through both loops on the hook. Work a double crochet into each of the remaining chains in the same way to complete the first row.

five When you reach the end of a row, finish by inserting the hook through the last two chains when pulling the first loop through, as shown.

six To start any subsequent rows of double crochet, turn the work so the loop on the hook is at the right-hand edge. Now make a 'turning' chain to take the yarn up to the correct height by drawing a loop through the loop on the hook to form a loose chain, as shown.

seven Inserting the hook through both loops at the top of the first stitch in the row below, work a double crochet into each double crochet of the previous row. Work following rows in the same way.

Treble crochet

Treble crochet is taller than double crochet. It results in a stitch that is more open and less dense, so it is a flexible, soft textile. It is worked in much the same way as double crochet, except that you wrap the yarn around the hook before beginning the stitch. And as it is taller, you begin by working a foundation chain to the required length and then inserting the hook into the fourth chain from the hook.

one Make a foundation chain to the length you require. Wrap the yarn around the hook as shown before inserting the hook into the fourth chain from the hook.

two Draw the yarn through. There are now three loops on the hook. Wrap the yarn around the hook once more, as shown.

three Draw the yarn through the first loop on the hook, leaving three loops on the hook.

four Wrap the around the hook again and draw the yarn through the first two loops, leaving two loops on the hook, as shown.

five Wrap the yarn around the hook and draw the yarn through the remaining two loops to complete the stitch, as shown. Wrap the yarn around the hook to begin the next treble. Work a treble crochet into each of the remaining chains in the same way to complete the row.

six At the end of the second and all subsequent rows, work the last stitch into the top of the three-chain at the edge – wrap the yarn around the hook and pull through the first loop, as shown.

seven Now wrap the yarn around the hook and pull the yarn through the first two loops. Wrap the yarn around and pull through the remaining two loops. Work all following rows in the same way. To start any subsequent rows of treble crochet, turn the work so the loop on the hook is at the right-hand edge. Now make a 'turning' chain to take the yarn up to the correct height by making three chain – this counts as the first stitch in the row. Miss the first stitch in the row below and work the first treble into the top of the next stitch.

Half treble

The two remaining basic crochet stitches are half treble and double treble. A half treble is slightly shorter than a treble, while a double treble is slightly taller. Try them out following the instructions given below and opposite.

one Make a foundation chain to the length required. Wrap the yarn around the hook before inserting the hook into the third chain from the hook, as shown.

two There are now three loops on the hook. Wrap the yarn around the hook again.

three Draw the yarn through all three loops on the hook to complete the half treble stitch. At the beginning of the second row, work two turning chains instead of three.

Double treble

one Make a foundation chain to the length required. Wrap the yarn twice around the hook as shown before inserting the hook into the fifth chain from the hook.

two Draw the yarn through two loops on the hook three times. At the beginning of the second row, work four turning chains instead of three.

Triple treble

This makes a very elongated treble stitch. It creates a light and delicate fabric, which is often used in lace patterns.

one Make a foundation chainto the length required. Wrap yarn round hook three times. Insert hook through work. Wrap yarn round hook. Draw yarn through. (Five loops on hook). Wrap yarn round hook and draw through first two loops. Repeat three times until one loop left on hook. Repeat as required.

Solomon's knot

A Solomon's Knot is a lengthened chain stitch locked with a double crochet stitch worked into its back loop.

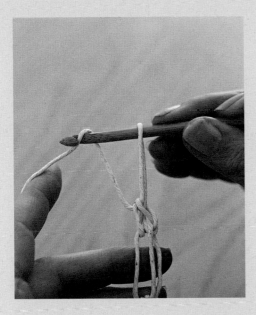

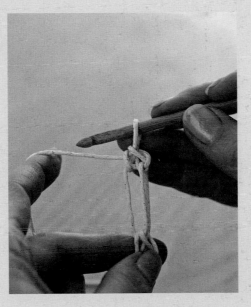

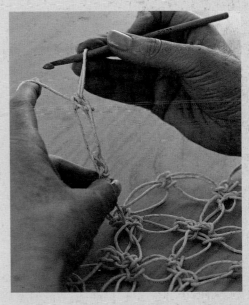

one Make one chain and lengthen the loop as required; wrap the yarn over the hook. Draw through the loop on the hook, keeping the single back thread of this long chain separate from the two front threads. Insert the hook under this single back thread and wrap the yarn again. Draw a loop through and wrap again.

two Draw through both loops on the hook to complete.

three It is necessary to work back into the 'knots' between the lengthened chains in order to make the classic Solomon's Knot fabric (see pages 80–3).

Working in rounds

Some circular pieces are worked in rounds rather than rows. The stitches may vary, but the basic technique is the same. To begin, make a ring of a few chain stitches as the foundation. The yarn thickness will determine how many chain stitches you make, but generally, for a hole at the centre that is drawn closed, about four or six chains will do.

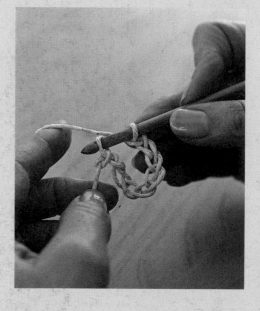

one Chain six and insert the hook through the first chain made. Wrap the yarn around the hook in the usual way.

two Draw the yarn through the chain and the loop on the hook as for a slip stitch. This forms a foundation ring of chain stitches.

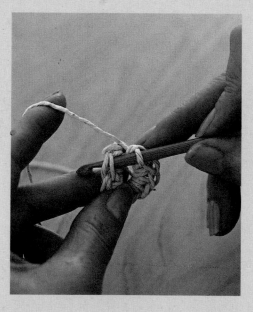

three If you are working double crochet into the ring, start by making one chain. (Make three chain if your first round is trebles, two for half treble or four for double trebles.) Inserting the hook into the ring, work as many stitches into the ring as required to fill the circle.

four To make a motif, continue working in rounds, building up rounds of stitches. Here, a second round of treble crochet is being worked into a first round of double crochet.

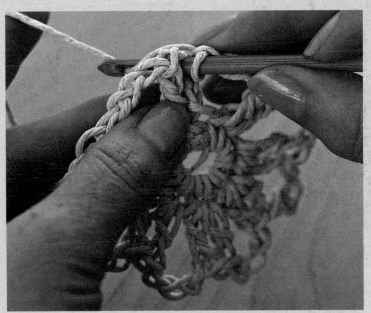

five To finish a round, join the round together with a slip stitch to the appropriate chain. Continue making rounds or finish off, as required.

Freeform crochet

A twist on the more traditional crochet, this is freeform crochet, freestyle crochet or couture crochet, as I like to call it. Individually designed and custom-made to measure especially for you or for your home, freeform crochet is, just as the name suggests, organic, with no fixed pattern or rules.

Freeform crochet is an endlessly interesting and innovative way of working. It requires a different approach to crochet from the more traditional methods, as it is much more creative, with no fixed pattern or rules. Basically, freeform crochet involves making an assortment of motifs, and even half motifs, and then linking them together in a random way to create a unique fabric.

Work a collection of various motifs – centres, rosettes, circles – as required. Work small extra groups of treble stitches grafted onto these motifs to make attractive, asymmetrical extensions. (A collection of interesting motifs are given in the patterns for the Molded Wire Mat on pages 86–9, the Freeform Table Runner on pages 104–107 and the Freeform Camisole on pages 154–9.) Make some half motifs, if required. (Again, instructions for some of these are given in the pattern for the Freeform Camisole on pages 154–9.)

Simply pin each finished motif haphazardly onto a paper template of your chosen shape. Using a pencil, draw in chain lines between the motifs to link them up as desired, leaving approximately 4–5cm between each motif. While the motifs are still pinned onto the paper template, crochet the linking chains, following the drawn lines, and adding and inserting extra groups of treble stitches at the crossover points of two or more chains. Join the chain to the next motif with a slip stitch and so on.

Appraise your work regularly by eye, and adjust as necessary, to create a completely one-off and very creative piece of crochet.

Basic

This selection of simple projects ranging from sumptuous throws, an elegant wrap and a cosy scarf, uses the most basic stitches, such as double crochet and treble crochet. Worked in textural materials such as tweed, mohair and leather, they reflect the natural elements of the earth. With a warming colour palette of autumnal chestnuts, leaf greens and lichen, these projects evoke memories of coastal holidays, country days out and family picnics.

Woven plaid throw

Unashamedly luxurious and extravagant, yet easy to make, this throw is worked in rich tweeds laced through with velvety chenilles. Its mellow colours are inspired by nature in the autumn, but this design would work equally well in summery brights. Bands of basic filet crochet have been worked in colourful wool tweeds, which are then woven with threads of chenille that are knotted to form a fringe edging. This design can be interpreted to include as many colours and textures as you like – use up yarns from 'end of line' bins or from your own stash – or simply work it in only two or three yarns to complement a particular interior scheme.

Making the Woven plaid throw

THROW SIZE
Approximately 190cm x 168cm

MATERIALS
Rowan Yorkshire Tweed Aran or a similar
weight yarn (see page 170) in four colours:
Colour A: 4 x 100g hanks in brown
Colour B: 2 x 100g hanks in oatmeal
Colour C: 4 x 100g hanks in purple
Colour D: 5 x 100g hanks in green
Rowan Chunky Cotton Chenille or a similar
weight yarn (see page 170) in seven colours:
Colour E: 1 x 100g ball in taupe
Colour F: 1 x 100g ball in dark green
Colour G: 1 x 100g ball in purple
Colour H: 1 x 100g ball in deep red
Colour J: 1 x 100g ball in lilac
Colour K: 1 x 100g ball in light green

Colour L: 1 x 100g ball in ecru
Hook size 6.00mm

STITCH SIZE
This throw has a tension of 12tr to 10cm
and 6 rows to 10cm measured over treble
crochet using a 6.00mm hook

TECHNIQUES USED
Treble crochet and joining in new yarns

For treble crochet: see page 16

TIP
Joining in a new yarn: Begin the last
treble crochet in the usual way, but change
to the new yarn when drawing the yarn
through to the last loop of the stitch. Leave
a long loose end of the old and new yarns

to weave in later or work over the ends for
several stitches before clipping them off.

METHOD
Foundation chain: Using colour A, chain 214.
Foundation row: Work 1tr into 6th chain
from hook [1 chain, miss 1 chain, 1tr in next
chain] repeat to end. Turn. [105 spaces.]
Row 1: Chain 4, [1tr into next treble,
1 chain] repeat to last space, miss 1 chain,
1tr in 4th of 5th chain. Turn.
Stripe pattern repeat
Continuing to repeat row 1 for stitch pattern,
but ending each row with last treble worked
into 3rd of 4 chain, work in stripes as follows:
Colour A: 5 rows
Colour B: 3 rows
Colour C: 5 rows

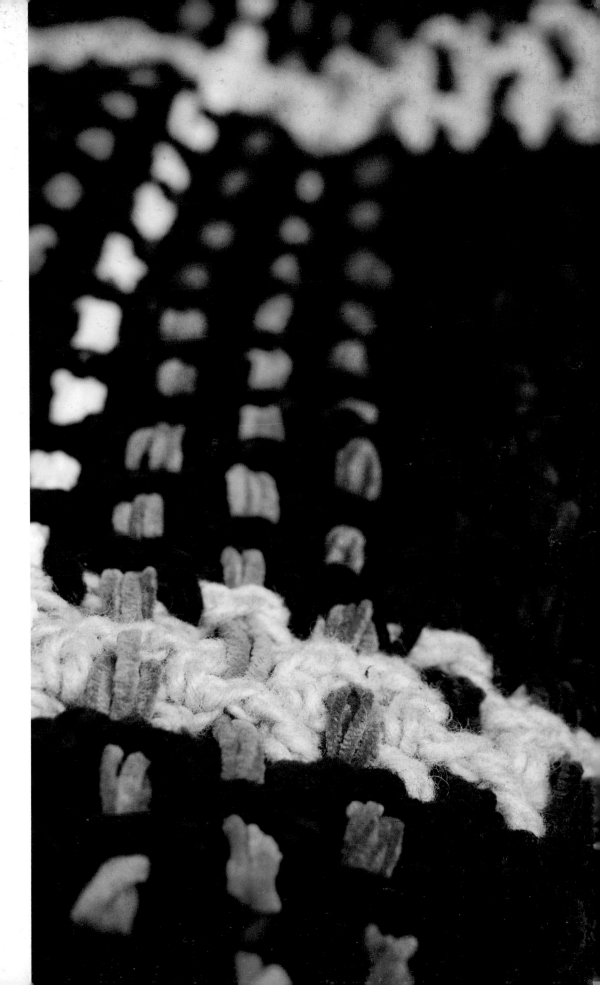

Colour D: 7 rows

Work 20-row stripe-pattern repeat 5 times in total.

Work 5 rows more in colour A, so that the throw ends with 5 rows A to match the beginning edge.

TO FINISH

Weave any loose ends into the work.

Lay the work out flat, then steam and press lightly.

Cut the chenille yarns into 610cm lengths.

Take three lengths, knot one end and use this knot to weave the yarn in and out of the holes made by the crochet.

Knot the lengths of chenille yarn at each end, leaving a tassel approximately 12cm long, and trim.

Button-trimmed scarf

This small scarf, made in basic double crochet, is worked in vegetal tones of tweed yarns softened with wisps of fine mohair. Crocheted in a random stripe sequence to blend the colours together for a hand dyed effect, the scarf is trimmed decoratively with assorted mother-of-pearl buttons that reflect the colours of the yarns.

Making the Button-trimmed scarf

SCARF SIZE
Approximately 19cm x 102cm

MATERIALS
Rowan Summer Tweed or a similar weight
yarn (see page 170) in five colours:
Colour A: 1 x 50g hank in dark grey
Colour B: 1 x 50g hank in moss green
Colour C: 1 x 50g hank in marl grey
Colour D: 2 x 50g hanks in oatmeal
Colour E: 1 x 50g hank in lime green
Rowan Kidsilk Haze or a similar light-weight
yarn (see page 170) in two colours:
Colour F: 1 x 25g ball in lime green
Colour G: 1 x 25g ball in olive green
Hook size 4.50mm
Approximately 40–60 assorted buttons
Sewing needle and thread

STITCH SIZE
This scarf has a tension of 8½ stitches and
15 rows to 10cm measured over pattern of
1dc, 1ch, using a 4.50mm hook.

TECHNIQUES USED
Double crochet and joining in new yarns

For double crochet: see page 14

TIP
Joining in a new yarn: Begin the last
double crochet in the usual way, but
change to the new yarn when drawing the
yarn through to the last loop of the stitch.
Leave a long loose end of the old and new
yarns to weave in later or work over the
ends for several stitches before clipping
them off.

METHOD
Foundation row: Using colours A and G
together, chain 34.
Row 1: Using colour A, 1dc in 4th chain
from hook [chain 1, miss 1 chain, 1dc in
next chain] repeat to end.
Row 2: Chain 2 [1dc in 1st chain space,
chain 1] repeat to end. Turn.
Stripe pattern repeat
Continuing to repeat row 2 for stitch
pattern, work in stripes starting with the
third row of colour A below the foundation
row (you have already worked the
foundation row and the first 2 rows in
colours A and G):
* Colours A and G: 1 row (foundation row)
Colour A: 9 rows
Colour B: 1 row

Colour A: 1 row
Colour B: 5 rows
Colours B and G: 3 rows
Colour C: 1 row
Colour B: 1 row
Colour C: 2 rows
Colour D: 1 row
Colour C: 1 row
Colour D: 4 rows
Colours E and G: 2 rows
Colour E: 6 rows
Colour D: 1 row
Colour E: 1 row
Colour D and F: 1 row **
Colour D with random rows of either
colour F or G: 81 rows
Repeat the stripe pattern in reverse, starting
from ** and working back to *.

TO FINISH
Weave any loose ends into the work.
Lay the work out flat, then steam and
press lightly.
Sew the buttons on randomly at both
ends of the scarf using the sewing thread.

Textured round cushion

The tweed yarn used to make this cushion is combined with silk to give an interesting texture that is very effective when crocheted. The muted natural hues are all so beautiful that it was hard to choose a single one, so instead I used small amounts of lots of colours. The cushion is worked in simple rounds of basic treble crochet, using colours in tonal bands, then finished with a spiral-stitch trim. This cushion is a very striking accessory for either a modern or traditional chair.

Making the Textured round cushion

CUSHION SIZE

Approximately 46cm in diameter

MATERIALS

Rowan Summer Tweed or a similar aran-weight yarn (see page 170) in eight colours:

Colour A: 1 x 50g hank in red

Colour B: 1 x 50g hank in burnt orange

Colour C: 1 x 50g hank in dark brown

Colour D: 1 x 50g hank in lime green

Colour E: 1 x 50g hank in purple

Colour F: 1 x 50g hank in red

Colour G: 1 x 50g hank in dark red

Colour H: 1 x 50g hank in mid brown

Hook size 4.50mm

46cm diameter cushion pad

STITCH SIZE

This cushion has a tension of 13 stitches and 6 rows to 10cm measured over treble crochet using a 4.50mm hook, but working to an exact tension is not essential (see Tips).

TECHNIQUES USED

Treble crochet, working in rounds and joining in new yarns

For treble crochet: see page 16
For working in rounds: see page 22

TIPS

Working in rounds: When you work in rounds, you never have to turn the fabric. The right side is always facing you.

Tension: Don't worry about tension too much! Because this cushion cover is made in circles, you can work your stitches in rounds until it is the required size.

Marking the beginning of a round: There is no need to mark the beginning of each round because of the colour changes.

Joining in a new yarn: Begin the last treble crochet in the usual way, but change to the new yarn when drawing the yarn through to the last loop of the stitch. Leave a long loose end of the old and new yarns to weave in later or work over the ends for several stitches before clipping them off.

Making a round cushion pad: Customise a square cushion pad by first chalking an 46cm circle on the pad. Then take each corner in turn, shake the stuffing to the middle, fold down the empty corners and stitch through both layers along the chalked line.

METHOD

Front and Back (make 2)

Foundation chain: Leaving a long, loose end and using colour A, chain 4 and join length of chain into ring by working a slip stitch into 1st chain made.

Round 1 (right side): Chain 3, work 11tr into ring, working over long, loose end. Join with a slip stitch into 3rd of first 3 chain. [12 trebles]. Change to colour B.

Round 2: Chain 3, 1tr into same stitch, [2tr into next treble] repeat to end. Join with a slip stitch into 3rd of first 3 chain. [24 trebles] Change to colour C.

Round 3: Chain 3, 1tr into same stitch, 1tr into next treble, [2tr into next treble, 1tr into next treble] repeat to end. Join with a slip stitch into 3rd of 1st 3 chain.

[36 trebles] Change to colour D.

Round 4: Chain 3, 1tr into same stitch, 1tr into each of next 2tr, [2tr into next treble, 1tr into each of next 2tr] repeat to end. Join with a slip stitch into 3rd of 1st 3 chain. [48 trebles] Change to colour E.

Round 5: Chain 3, 1tr into same stitch, 1tr into each of next 3tr, [2tr into next treble, 1tr into each of next 3tr] repeat to end. Join with a slip stitch into 3rd of 1st 3 chain. [60 trebles] Change to colour F. Continue in rounds, increasing 12 stitches on every round by working one more stitch between each increase and changing colour each time until round 16 has been worked. Fasten off.

Repeat eight colour pattern twice or add more rounds to achieve the required size.

TO FINISH

Weave any loose ends into the wrong side of the work. Lay the pieces out flat, then steam and press lightly. Join together as follows:

Place the pieces together with the wrong sides facing each other, line up the stitches along the outside edge and pin together. Using colour A, work a row of dc around the edge until the opening is just large enough to enclose the cushion pad. Insert and finish the edging by continuing with dc to the end of the round. Join with a slip stitch.

Next round: Chain 3, 1dc into each of the 1st 2 chain, then slip stitch into 1st dc, [1dc into next 2dc, 3 chain, 1dc into each of 1st 2 chain, slip stitch in same dc] repeat to end. Fasten off and weave in the end.

Beaded cobweb wrap

A wrap is the perfect accessory, being both practical and stylish. They are simple to wear, can be carried easily and pack well. Although this wrap is made in whisper-fine silk mohair, it will keep you warm and comfortable. Constructed in a basic open stitch that is quick to make, light and airy, it is a great project for the beginner, as it grows very quickly. The tiny glass beads are easy to crochet in along the edge and add an extra hint of luxury.

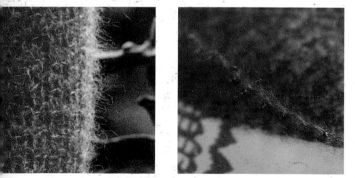

Making the Beaded cobweb wrap

WRAP SIZE
Approximately 165cm x 75cm

MATERIALS
6 x 25g balls of Rowan Kidsilk Haze or a
similar light-weight yarn (see page 170)
Hook size 6.00mm
Approximately 250 2.00mm glass beads

STITCH SIZE
This wrap has a tension of 7½ stitches and
15 rows to 10cm measured over double
crochet using a 6.00m hook.

TECHNIQUES USED
Double crochet and crocheting in beads
(see pattern)

For double crochet: see page 14

METHOD
Foundation chain: Chain 236.
Row 1: Work 1dc in 4th chain from hook,
[1 chain, miss 1 chain, 1dc into next chain]
repeat to end.
Row 2: 2 chain [counts as 1st dc and 1st 1
chain space] miss 1st dc and work 1dc into
1st 1 chain space, [1 chain, miss next dc,
1dc into next 1 chain space] repeat to end
working last dc into chain space at edge.
Turn.
Repeat row 2 until work measures 75cm.
Fasten off.

TO FINISH
Weave any loose ends into the work.
Before starting to work, thread half the
beads onto the yarn.

Work 1 row of dc, adding a bead on every
stitch, across both short ends of the wrap.
Adding a bead in double crochet: Insert
the hook through the stitch of the previous
row in the usual way, yarn round hook and
draw a loop through. Then slide the bead
close to the work, yarn round hook and
draw through both loops at the same time
pushing the bead firmly on top of the stitch
in the previous row. Weave in the yarn ends
on each short edge.

Leather tote bag

Leather is great to crochet with, although it takes a little time to get used to its particular characteristics. Leather thonging is available in widths from 0.50–5.00mm. The maximum size for ease of crochet is probably 2.00mm; thicker weights can be more difficult to work with, although they make great bag handles.

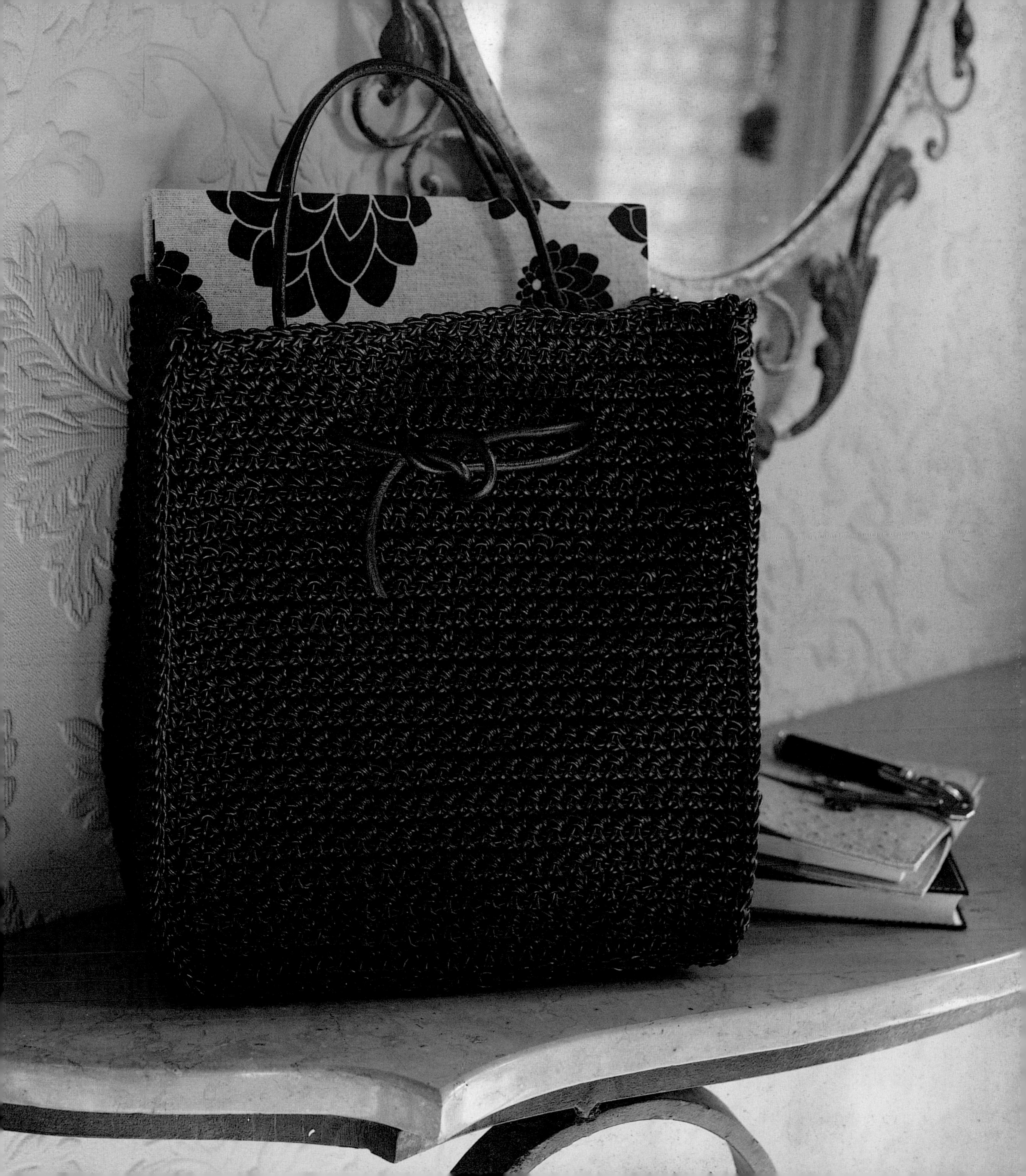

Making the Leather tote bag

BAG SIZE
Approximately 29cm x 25cm

MATERIALS
7 x 50m balls 1.50mm-thick round leather thonging or alternative yarn (see page 170)
Hook sizes 5.00mm and 6.00mm
170cm 5.00mm-thick round leather thonging, for handles

STITCH SIZE
This bag has a tension of 11dc and 14 rows to 10cm measured over double crochet using a 6.00m hook

TECHNIQUES USED
Double crochet

For double crochet: see page 14

TIP
Leather: Leather is quite hard on the hands, so when working with it, concentrate on just one stitch at a time. Warm the leather in your hands as you work to soften it. It can become sticky, too, so a little talcum powder on the hook may assist in pulling it through.

METHOD
Front and Back (make 2)
Foundation chain: Using 6.00mm hook, chain 29.
Row 1: 1dc in 2nd chain from hook, 1dc in each chain to end. Turn. [28 stitches.]
Row 2: 1 chain, dc to end. Turn.
Repeat row 2 until work measures 29cm. Fasten off.

Gusset
Foundation chain: Using 6.00mm hook, chain 12.
Row 1: As row 1 given for Front and Back. [11 stitches.]
Row 2: As row 2 given for Front and Back until work measures 83cm. Fasten off.

TO FINISH
Weave any loose ends into the work. Attach the gusset to three edges of the Front by working dc through both layers using 5.00mm hook, working 3dc into the corners, so that the seam is on the outside. Fasten off. Weave in ends. Repeat with the Back. Thread the thicker leather through the Front and Back of the bag as shown, then knot securely to make the bag handles.

Textured aran throw

I love the simplicity of crocheted textures. Just two basic stitches are used to make this indulgent merino wool throw. Each stitch is used separately to work oversized squares that are alternated to create strips, which are then sewn together to assemble the throw. Although the finished throw is quite heavy, because you only work one stitch at a time in crochet there is no weight to support while making it; in this respect, crochet is unlike knitting, where the weight of the work is carried on the needles at all times. This gorgeous throw would delight anyone as a beautiful housewarming or wedding gift – make it in classic ecru or add in a contemporary accent colour.

Making the Textured aran throw

THROW SIZE

Approximately 190cm x 190cm

MATERIALS

43 x 100g balls Rowan Polar or a similar
aran-weight wool yarn (see page 170)
Hook sizes 7.00mm and 8.00mm
Large sewing needle

STITCH SIZE

This throw has a tension of 9 stitches and
8 rows to 10cm measured over half treble
crochet worked with an 8.00mm hook

TECHNIQUES USED

Double crochet and half treble crochet

For double crochet: see page 14

For half treble crochet: see page 18

TIP

Stitch pattern: When making the bobble
squares, take care to check that you have
all the bobbles on the same side of the
work and that they are all made with the
wrong side of the work facing you.

METHOD

Foundation chain: Using 8.00mm hook,
chain 37 loosely.

Row 1: 1dc in 2nd chain from hook, 1dc in
each chain to end. [36 stitches.] Turn with
1 chain.

Bobble square

Row 2 (wrong side): 1dc in next stitch,
[1 double treble, 1dc] to last stitch, 1dc,
chain 1. Turn.

Row 3 (right side): dc to end, chain 1. Turn.

Repeat these last two rows until work
measures 38cm.

Plain square

Continue working the strip in half treble
crochet turning each row with 2 chain for
a further 38cm.

With right side of the work facing for the
next row and starting with row 3, work
another 38cm bobble square.

Next, work another 38cm plain square
followed by another 38cm bobble square.
Fasten off.

You have now completed one strip of
five squares.

Make another two strips in the same way
that both start and end with bobble
squares. Then make two more strips that
both start and finish with plain squares.

To start a 38cm plain square, chain 38 and

work 1 half treble in 3rd chain from hook, then half treble to end. [36 stitches.]

TO FINISH

Weave any loose ends into the work.
Join alternating strips together with small, neat oversewn stitches.
Using hook size 7.00mm, work 3 rows of dc all round the edge, working 3dc into each corner, 1dc into each stitch along top and bottom and 1dc into each row along sides. Make sure that the work is not puckering up as you go. Fasten off.
Weave in any remaining loose ends.

Timeless

Quintessentially elegant, covetable and collectable pieces that hark back to the traditions of crochet while simplifying and updating them for the modern era. Motifs worked in the round are synonymous with the craft of crochet, so here I have created a classic patchwork throw using the simplest shape. Crochet also lends itself superbly to fine lace and filet work, so included are a selection of my favourite pieces from lace edgings for pillowslips and bedlinen to a filet work cushion that is sheer perfection.

String stool

Natural string has a great matt colour, gives an interesting texture and stitch clarity, and is great for projects around the home. Although it requires a little more patience to work with initially as it is not a conventional yarn, the results are striking. This simple stool is made from a round motif top and bottom with an easy cluster stitch section in the middle. Seek out old pouffes from thrift stores to recover or alternatively use pre-cut foam from hardware shops.

Making the String stool

STOOL SIZE

Approximately 18cm high x 38cm in diameter, but measurements can be easily adjusted as required

MATERIALS

9 x 89m balls thick parcel string (from hardware or stationery stores, see page 170)
Hook size 4.00mm
Large sewing needle
Fabric to cover base (optional)

STITCH SIZE

This stool has a tension of 6½ clusters and 7 rows to 10cm measured over cluster pattern rows using a 4.00mm hook, but working to an exact tension is not essential (see Tips).

TECHNIQUES USED

Double crochet, double treble crochet and working in rounds

For double crochet: see page 14

For double treble crochet: see page 19

For working in rounds: see page 22

TIPS

Working in rounds: When you work in rounds, you never have to turn the fabric. The right side is always facing you.

Tension: Don't worry about tension too much! Because this stool cover is made in circles, you can work your stitches in a spiral until it is the required size.

Marking the beginning of a round: Mark the beginning of each round to make it easier to keep your place.

METHOD

Top and centre (worked as one piece)

Foundation chain: Leaving a long loose end, chain 8 and join length of chain into ring by working a slip stitch into 1st chain made.

Round 1: Chain 2 to count as 1st dc, work 15dc into circle. Join with a slip stitch into 2nd of 1st 2 chain. [16 stitches.]

Round 2: Chain 4 to count as 1st double treble, 1 double treble into next dc, * chain 4, 2 double treble, repeat from * to end, chain 4. Join with a slip stitch into 4th of 1st 4 chain.

Round 3: Slip stitch into next double treble and into 1st 4 chain space, chain 4, 5 double treble into same space, * chain 3, 6 double treble into next space, repeat from *

hook, insert hook between next 2 double trebles, draw through a loop, yarn round hook, draw through 2 loops) 3 times in the same space, yarn round hook, draw through 4 loops, chain 1, miss next space, repeat from * to end, omitting last 1 chain of repeat. Join with a slip stitch into 3rd of 3 chain. [80 clusters.]

Round 11: Chain 3, * 1 cluster in chain between clusters of previous row, chain 1, repeat from * to end and join with a slip stitch into 3rd of 3 chain.

Repeat round 11 until work measures approximately 24cm or required length. Adjust the length here to fit the height of your pouffe, less 2.5cm to allow cover to fit tightly. Fasten off.

Base

Work Rounds 1 to 9 as given for Top. Fasten off.

TO FINISH

If necessary, cover the foam inner with fabric. Cut two circles to the size of the top and base, adding a 1.5cm seam allowance all the way around, and cut a length to the size of the middle section, adding a 1.5cm seam allowance all the way round. Sew the middle section to the top circle. Sew the middle section seam. Turn right side out and slip the sewn cover over the foam inner. Sew the bottom circle to the middle section to enclose, using small neat hand stitches. Slip the crocheted top and middle section over and again slip stitch the crochet bottom to finish. Sew in any yarn ends to the wrong side of the work.

to end, chain 3. Join with a slip stitch into 4th of 4 chain.

Round 4: Chain 4, 1 double treble into same place as last slip stitch, * 4 double treble, 2 double treble into next double treble, 4 chain, 2 double treble into next double treble, repeat from * to end, omitting 2 double treble at end of last repeat. Join with a slip stitch into 4th of 4 chain.

Round 5: Chain 4, 7 double treble leaving last loop of each double treble on hook, yarn round hook and draw through all loops on hook, * chain 8, 1dc into next space, chain 8, 8 double treble leaving last loop of each double treble on hook, yarn round hook and draw through all loops on hook – called double treble cluster – repeat from * ending with 8 chain, 1dc into next space, 8 chain. Join with a slip stitch into

top of 1st double treble cluster.

Round 6: Slip stitch into each of next 4 chain, 1dc into loop, * chain 9, 1dc into next loop, repeat from * ending with 9 chain. Join with a slip stitch into 1st dc.

Round 7: Slip stitch into each of next 3 chain, chain 4, 4 double treble into same loop, * chain 5, 5 double treble into next loop, repeat from * ending with 5 chain. Join with a slip stitch into 4th of 1st chain.

Round 8: 1dc into same place as last slip stitch, 1dc into each of next 4 double trebles, * 5dc into next space, 1dc into each of next 5 trebles, repeat from * ending with 5dc into last space. Join with a slip stitch into 1st dc.

Round 9: Chain 4, 1 double treble into every dc to end. Join with a slip stitch into top of chain. [160 double trebles.]

Round 10: Chain 3, * 1 cluster (yarn round

Satin lingerie case

This sumptuous lingerie case is crocheted in a cluster stitch that creates a firm fabric with an attractive texture that gives a vintage feel. It is made very simply in a long strip, which is then folded and stitched. The natural finish of the scallop stitch gives a lovely edge detail. The bag is lined in toning satin material for pure indulgence and a big chocolate bow attached adds a further touch of luxury. Make a larger bag for pyjamas and a smaller one for jewellery or favourite accessories.

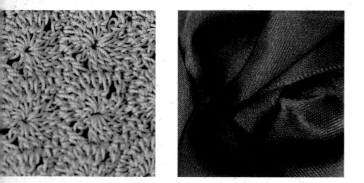

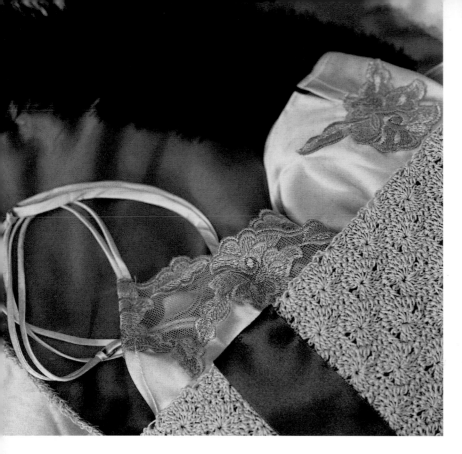

Making the Satin lingerie case

CASE SIZE
Approximately 20cm x 27cm

MATERIALS
3 x 50g balls Coats Aida or similar no. 5
mercerised cotton yarn (see page 170)
Hook size 1.75mm
Fabric for lining, approximately 60cm x 30cm
2m satin ribbon, 3.5cm wide

STITCH SIZE
This pillow has a tension of 3 pattern
repeats to 9cm and 8 rows to 10cm
measured over stitch pattern.

TECHNIQUES USED
Double crochet, treble crochet and
cluster stitch (see pattern)

For double crochet: see page 14

For treble crochet: see page 16

METHOD
Cluster stitch
Cluster: Work [yarn over hook, insert hook,
yarn over hook, draw loop through, yarn
over hook, draw through 2 loops] over the
number of stitches indicated, yarn over
hook, draw through all loops on hook.
Row 1 (wrong side): 1dc into 2nd chain
from hook, 1dc into next chain, * miss 3
chain, 7tr into next chain, miss 3 chain, 1dc
into each of next 3 chain, repeat from * to
last 4 chain, miss 3 chain, 4tr into last
chain. Turn.
Row 2: Chain 1, 1dc into 1st stitch, 1dc
into next stitch, * chain 3, 1 cluster over

next 7 stitches, chain 3, 1dc into each of
next 3 stitches, repeat from * to last 4
stitches, chain 3, 1 cluster over last 4
stitches, miss turning chain. Turn.
Row 3: Chain 3 [count as 1tr], 3tr into 1st
stitch, * miss 3 chain, 1dc into each of next
3dc, miss 3 chain, 7tr into loop which
closed next cluster, repeat from * to end
finishing with miss 3 chain, 1dc into each
of last 2dc, miss turning chain. Turn.
Row 4: Chain 3 [count as 1tr], miss 1st
stitch, 1 cluster over next 3 stitches, * chain
3, 1dc into each of next 3 stitches, chain 3,
1 cluster over next 7 stitches, repeat from *
finishing with chain 3, 1dc into next stitch,
1dc into top of turning chain. Turn.
Row 5: Chain 1, 1dc into each of 1st 2dc,
* miss 3 chain, 7tr into loop which closed

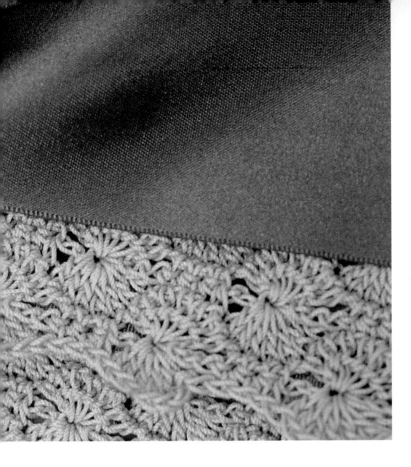

next cluster, miss 3 chain, 1dc into each of next 3dc, repeat from * ending miss 3 chain, 4tr into top of turning chain. Turn. Repeat rows 2, 3, 4 and 5.

CASE

Foundation chain: Chain 97.
Follow the Cluster stitch 4-row repeat pattern until work measures 55cm or required length, finishing on a row 5.

TO MAKE UP THE CASE

With right sides together, fold in 18cm at one end to make the pocket, leaving 19cm to create the flap. Pin and tack the two side seams. Stitch. Turn right side out.
Lay a length of ribbon all the way around the case, approximately 6cm from the left hand edge. Fold the ribbon over the inside pocket edge (this will eventually be hidden by the lining).
On the outside flap, stop the ribbon just short of the scalloped edge and neatly finish it by turning the end under (this will be hidden by the bow). Pin or tack into position. Secure using small, neat hand stitches.

TO MAKE THE LINING

Cut a piece of lining fabric to the same size as the crocheted case, adding a 1.5cm seam allowance all the way around.
With right sides together, fold in 19.5cm at one end to make the pocket, leaving 17.5cm to create the flap. Pin and tack the two side seams. Stitch.
Turn under 1.5cm on each unhemmed edge of the lining and press.
Insert the lining into the crocheted case and pin or tack into position. Stitch the lining to the crocheted case around the pocket opening and flap using small, neat hand stitches.

TO FINISH

Take a length of satin ribbon and tie it into a large bow. Place the bow on top of the ribbon sash, just above the scalloped edge. Pin or tack into position. Secure with small, neat hand stitches.

Lacy pillowslip edgings

Decorate vintage, heirloom or crisp new pillowslips and sheets with these very easy lace edgings to lend a personal touch to the bedroom. There are three – a pretty lace, a little point and an ornate scallop shell. They are worked in strips so are much easier to make than having to pick up from the fabric itself. These are made in pristine white mercerised cotton, however they would look very pretty in soft colours to enhance faded old pillowslips, perhaps handed down from your grandmother or sourced from favourite thrift store.

Making the Lacy pillowslip edgings

EDGING SIZE

To fit pillowslips approximately 80cm long and 50cm wide, but measurements can be easily adjusted as required

MATERIALS

Approximately 50g Yeomans Cotton Cannele or similar 4-ply mercerised cotton yarn (see page 170) each for Lace Edging and Lace Point Edging and approximately 100g for Scallop Shell Edging
Hook size 2.00mm

TECHNIQUES USED

Double crochet and treble crochet

For double crochet: see page 14

For treble crochet: see page 16

TIPS

Tension: Don't worry about tension too much! Because these edgings are made in strips, you can work extra stitches until the edging is the required size.

Lace edging

STITCH SIZE

This edging has a tension of 4 pattern repeats to 7cm, but working to an exact tension is not essential (see Tips).

METHOD

Foundation chain: Chain 11.
Foundation row: 2tr in 7th chain from hook, 3 chain, 2tr in next chain, miss next 2 chain, 1tr in last chain. Turn.

Row 1: Chain 5, 2tr 3 chain 2tr in 3 chain space. Turn.
Row 2: Chain 6, 2tr 3 chain 2tr in 3 chain space, 2 chain, 1tr in 3rd of 5 chain. Turn. Repeat rows 1 and 2 until work measures 80cm or length required, ending with row 1. Do not turn.

Edging: Chain 3, 1dc in base of last treble, * 3 chain, [1tr, 3 chain] 3 times in 6 chain space at end of row, miss next row end, 1dc in 3 chain space at centre of next row, repeat from * to end, omitting 3 chain and 1dc at end of last repeat. Fasten off.

Scallop shell edging

STITCH SIZE

This edging has a tension of 1 pattern

repeat to 7cm, but working to an exact tension is not essential (see Tips).

METHOD

Foundation chain: Chain 8 and join length of chain into ring by working a slip stitch into 1st chain made.

Row 1: 3 chain, 8tr into ring, 4 chain. Turn.

Row 2: 1tr into 2nd tr, * 1 chain, 1tr, repeat from * 6 times, 5 chain. Turn.

Row 3: 1tr into 1st space, * 2 chain, 1tr, repeat from * 6 times, 6 chain. Turn.

Row 4: 1tr into 1st space, * 3 chain, 1tr, repeat from * 6 times, 1 chain. Turn.

Row 5: * 1dc 3tr 1dc into next space, repeat from * 7 times, 8 chain. Turn.

Row 6: 1dc into centre treble of 1st group of 3, 3 chain. Turn.

Row 7: 8tr into space, 4 chain. Turn.

Row 8: 1tr into 2nd treble, * 1 chain, 1tr into next stitch, repeat from * 6 times, 1dc into centre treble of next group of 3 on previous scallop, 5 chain. Turn.

Row 9: As row 3.

Row 10: 1tr into 1st space, * 3 chain, 1tr into next space, repeat from * 6 times, 1dc into centre treble of next group of 3 on previous scallop, 1 chain. Turn.

Repeat rows 5 to 10 inclusive until a corner is required, ending with a row 10.

Shape corner

Row 1: 1dc 3tr 1dc into each space, 6 chain. Turn.

Row 2: 1dc into centre treble of 1st group of 3, 3 chain. Turn.

Row 3: 12tr into space, 4 chain. Turn.

Repeat row 8, row 3 and row 10, repeating instructions from * 10 times in each row.

Row 7: 1dc 3tr 1dc into each space, 8 chain. Turn.

This completes the corner.

Repeat rows 6 to 10 inclusive of shell edge once, then repeat rows 5 to 10 inclusive until another corner is required.

Continue working in this way until edging is the required length to fit the pillowslip, ending with row 5, omitting final 8 chain. Fasten off leaving a long thread.

Join last 3 clusters worked to 1st shell worked.

The sample shown was made with 6 shells, 1 corner, 7 shells, 1 corner, 12 shells, 1 corner, 7 shells, 1 corner, 6 shells, finishing with a row 5.

Lace point edging

STITCH SIZE

This edging has a tension of 5 pattern repeats to 8cm, but working to an exact tension is not essential (see Tips).

METHOD

Foundation chain: Chain 103.

Row 1 (right side): 1dc into 2nd chain from hook, * 6 chain, 1dc into 3rd chain from hook, 3tr (one point made), miss 3 chain, 1dc into next chain, repeat from * to end. Fasten off leaving a long thread.

To make this edging to the required length to fit the pillowslip, adjust the number of chains in the foundation chain. If it is too long when you have finished working the points, undo the extra ones.

TO FINISH

Weave any loose ends into the wrong side of the work. Lay the work out flat, then steam and press lightly.

Place the edging around edge of pillowslip, pin and sew into position using small, neat hand stitches.

Scented pillow

This scented pillow is the perfect handmade gift: small, simple and quick to crochet, yet useful and especially pretty. Hang it in a closet, place it in a lingerie drawer or simply hook it on a door handle. This pillow is made in crisp, fine white cotton and worked in filet crochet for contrast, which reveals an organza pillow filled with fragrant dried lavender. The pillow is tied with silk ribbon and set off by a heart-shaped mother-of-pearl button. Personalise your pillow to create something unique for a friend: embroider or bead, edge or embellish, or use rose petals instead of lavender for an aunt or perhaps try rosemary for a keen gardener.

Making the Scented pillow

PILLOW SIZE
Approximately 15cm x 10cm

MATERIALS
1 x 50g ball Coats Aida or similar no. 10
mercerised cotton yarn (see page 170)
Hook size 1.25mm
Button or trim of choice
Fine satin ribbon, 3mm wide
Fabric for pillow, such as organza,
approximately 18cm x 23cm
Sewing needle and thread
Dried lavender, rose petals or rosemary for
pillow filling

STITCH SIZE
This pillow has a tension of 10 stitches and
5 rows to 2.5cm measured over treble
crochet, but working to an exact gauge is
not essential (see Tips).

TECHNIQUES USED
Treble crochet, filet crochet and working
with charts (see pattern).

For treble crochet: see page 16

TIPS
Tension: Don't worry about tension too
much! If your pillow cover ends up a bit
bigger or smaller than the size given here,
just adjust the size of the pillow form.
Filet crochet charts: Filet crochet
instructions are usually charted. The blank
squares on the chart represent 'spaces' in
the filet and the squares with a symbol in
them represent the solid 'blocks' of trebles.

To follow a filet chart, read the odd-
numbered rows from right to left and the
even-numbered rows from left to right.
From this basic filet technique many
different patterns can be designed.

METHOD
Foundation row: Leaving a long loose
end, chain 68.
Row 1: Work 1tr in 8th chain from hook to
make 1st 'space', * 2 chain, miss 2 chain,
1tr, repeat from * to end. Turn. [21 spaces.]
Row 2: Chain 5, 1tr into top of treble in
row below, * 2 chain, 1tr, repeat from * to
end, working last tr in 3rd chain of previous
row. Turn.
Continue with row 3 of the chart, working
'blocks' and 'spaces' in this way.

'spaces' in this way until Row 16 has been completed.

For the pillow back, continue to work 16 rows of 1tr in each stitch. [63 stitches.] Fasten off.

TO MAKE THE PILLOW

With wrong sides together, fold fabric in half lengthwise and sew along two sides leaving 1.5cm seam allowance.

Turn right side out and fill with dried lavender, roses or other scented filling of your choice.

Turn in ends of open side by 1.5cm and sew with small, neat hand stitches to close.

TO FINISH

Weave any loose ends into the wrong side of the work. Lay the work out flat, then steam and press lightly.

With wrong sides together, fold pillow cover in half lengthwise. Rejoin yarn at one corner and working through both layers, working 2dc into each space and 4dc into each corner, work around three sides of the bag. Fasten off.

Insert scented pillow.

Add ribbons 8.5cm apart and tie bag together with piece of ribbon simply threaded through both sides.

Sew on a decorative button in the centre of the pillow front.

KEY

= block

= space

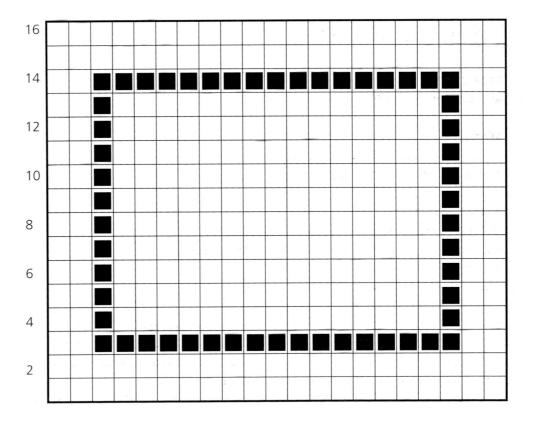

Filet lace cushion

Every modern and traditional boudoir deserves a pile of sumptuous cushions to add both comfort and glamour. Worked in patterns of doubles and trebles this lace cushion, made here in crisp mercerised cotton will add a little touch of romance to any room. The lace square is backed with white linen for added contrast and timeless appeal, but alternatively make it in girly pastels or gunmetal greens for a more contemporary setting or living space.

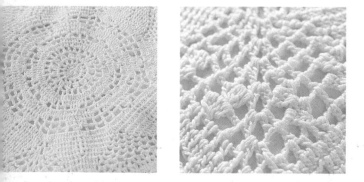

Making the Filet lace cushion

CUSHION SIZE

Approximately 40cm x 40cm

MATERIALS

125g Yeoman's Cotton Cannele or similar
4-ply mercerised cotton (see page 170)
Hook size 1.50mm
Approximately 1m linen, for cushion back
Sewing needle and thread
40cm x 40cm cushion pad

STITCH SIZE

This cushion has a tension of 13 rows to
10cm measured over filet lace pattern, but
working to an exact gauge is not essential
(see Tips).

TECHNIQUES USED

Double crochet, treble crochet, working in
rounds and cluster stitches (see pattern).

For double crochet: see page 14

For treble crochet: see page 16

For working in rounds: see page 22

TIPS

Tension: Don't worry about tension too
much! If your cushion cover ends up a bit
bigger or smaller than the size given here,
just adjust the size of the cushion pad or,
as this cushion cover is made in rounds,
you can work your stitches in rounds until
it is the required size.

Working in rounds: When you work in
rounds, you never have to turn the fabric.
The right side is always facing you.

Marking the beginning of a round:
Mark the beginning of each round to make
it easier to keep your place.

METHOD

Cluster stitches

Treble Cluster: Work a treble into each of
the next 3/5/6 stitches or as in Round 3
into a 2 chain space leaving the last loop
of each treble on the hook. Yarn over hook
and draw through all loops on the hook.

Double Treble Cluster: Work a double
treble into each of the next 5 stitches
leaving the last loop of each double treble
on the hook. Yarn over hook and draw
through all loops on the hook.

Base ring: Chain 6 and join length of chain into ring by working a slip stitch into 1st chain made.

Round 1: Chain 3 (count as 1tr), work 15tr into ring, slip stitch to 3rd chain.

Round 2: Chain 5 (count as 1tr, 2 chain), [1tr into next tr, 2 chain] 15 times, slip stitch to 3rd chain.

Round 3: Slip stitch into 1st 2 chain space, [3 treble cluster, 3 chain] in every space, slip stitch to top of 1st treble cluster.

Round 4: Slip stitch into 1st 2 chain space, 5 chain (count as 1tr, 2 chain), [1tr into top of treble cluster, 2 chain, 1tr into next 2 chain space, 2 chain] repeat to end. Join with slip stitch to 3rd chain. [32 spaces.]

Round 5: Slip stitch into 1st 2 chain space, 3 chain (count as 1st tr), [3tr in each space] repeat to end. Join with slip stitch to 3rd chain. [96 trebles.]

Round 6: Chain 5 (count as 1st tr, 2 chain) * 1tr, 2 chain, miss 1tr, 4tr, 1 chain, miss 1tr, 4tr, 2 chain, repeat from * to end. Join with slip stitch to 3rd chain.

Round 7: Chain 6 (count as 1st tr, 3 chain), [1tr, 3 chain] twice, * miss next tr, 5 treble cluster over next 5 stitches (count chain space as one stitch), 3 chain, miss next tr, [1tr, 3 chain] 3 times, repeat from * working only 1tr, 3 chain at end of last repeat at end of round. Join with slip stitch to 3rd chain.

Round 8: Chain 3 (count as 1st tr), * 3tr in 1st space, 1tr in next tr, [4tr in next space] twice, 1tr in next tr, 3tr in next space, repeat from * to end of round. Join with slip stitch to 3rd chain.

Round 9: Chain 6 (count as 1tr, 3 chain), * miss 2tr, 6tr, 1 chain, 6tr, 3 chain, ** miss 1tr, 1tr between next 2 tr, 3 chain, miss 3tr, 6tr, 1 chain, repeat from * ending last

repeat at **. Join with slip stitch to 3rd chain.

Round 10: Chain 6 (count as 1tr, 3 chain), 1tr in next tr, * miss 2tr, 3tr, 1 chain, 3tr, 3 chain, miss 2tr, ** [1tr in next tr, 3 chain] 3 times, repeat from * ending last repeat at **, 1tr, 1 chain. Join with slip stitch to 3rd chain.

Round 11: Chain 6 (count as 1tr, 3 chain), [1tr in next tr, 3 chain] twice, * 5 treble cluster over next 5 stitches counting chain space as one stitch, 3 chain, ** [1tr in next tr, 3 chain] 5 times, repeat from *, ending last repeat at **, [1tr in next tr, 3 chain] twice. Join with slip stitch to 3rd chain.

Round 12: Slip stitch into 1st space, 3 chain (count as 1 tr), 2tr in same space, * 1tr in next tr, 4tr in next space, 1tr in next tr, 3tr in next space, 1tr in top of cluster, 3tr in next space, 1tr in next tr, 4tr in next space, 1tr in next tr, ** [3tr in next space] twice, repeat from * ending last repeat at **, 3tr in next space. Join with slip stitch to 3rd chain.

Round 13: Chain 4 (count as 1 double treble), 1 double treble, 3 chain, 2 double treble in same place, * miss 2 stitches, 10tr, 1 chain, miss 1 stitch, 10tr, 4 chain, miss 2 stitches, 1dc between next 2 stitches, 4 chain, miss 2 stitches, 10tr, 1 chain, miss 1 stitch, 10tr, miss 2 stitches, ** [2 double treble, 3 chain, 2 double treble] between next 2 stitches, repeat from * ending last repeat at **. Join with slip stitch to 4th chain.

Round 14: Slip stitch into 3 chain space, 4 chain (count as 1st double treble), [2 double treble, 3 chain, 2 double treble] in this space, 1 chain, * 1 double treble between next 2 stitches, miss 2 stitches, 9tr, 1 chain, 9tr, miss 1 stitch, [4 chain, dc in

loop] twice, 4 chain, miss 1 stitch, 9tr, 1 chain, 9tr, miss 1 stitch, 1 double treble between next 2 stitches, 1 chain, ** [2 double treble, 3 chain, 2 double treble] in 3 chain loop, 1 chain, repeat from * ending last repeat at **. Join with slip stitch to 4th chain.

Round 15: Slip stitch into 3 chain space, 4 chain (count as 1st double treble), * [2 double treble, 3 chain, 2 double treble] in this space, [1 chain, 1 double treble between next 2 stitches] twice, miss next 2 stitches, 8tr, 1 chain, 8tr, miss next stitch, [4 chain, dc in next loop] three times, 4 chain, miss 1 stitch, 8tr, 1 chain, 8tr, miss 2 stitches, [1 double treble between next 2 stitches, 1 chain] twice, repeat from * to end of round. Join with slip stitch to 4th chain.

Round 16: Slip stitch into 3 chain space, 4 chain (count as 1st double treble), * [2 double treble, 3 chain, 2 double treble] in this space, miss 1 stitch, [1 chain, 1 double treble in next stitch] twice, 1 chain, 1 double treble in next space, miss next 2 stitches, 14tr, miss 1 stitch, [4 chain, dc in next loop] 4 times, 4 chain, miss next stitch, 14tr, miss 2 stitches, 1 double treble in next space, 1 chain, [1 double treble, 1 chain in next stitch] twice, miss next stitch, repeat from * to end of round. Join with slip stitch to 4th chain.

Round 17: Slip stitch into 3 chain space, 4 chain (count as 1st double treble), * [2 double treble, 3 chain, 2 double treble] in this space, miss next stitch, [1 chain, 1 double treble in next stitch] 3 times, 1 chain, 1 double treble in next space, miss next 2 stitches, 12tr, miss 1tr, [4 chain, 1dc in next loop] 5 times, 4 chain, miss next stitch, 12tr, miss 2 stitches, 1 double treble

in next space, 1 chain, [1 double treble, 1 chain in next stitch] 3 times, miss next stitch, repeat from * to end of round. Join with slip stitch to 4th chain.

Round 18: Slip stitch into 3 chain space, 4 chain (count as 1st treble), [2 double treble, 3 chain, 2 double treble] in this space, miss next stitch, [1 chain, 1 double treble in next stitch] 4 times, 1 chain, 1 double treble in next space, miss next 2 stitches, 10tr, miss 1 stitch, [4 chain, 1dc in next loop] 6 times, 4 chain, miss next stitch, 10tr, miss 2 stitches, 1 double treble in next space, 1 chain, [1 double treble, 1 chain in next stitch] 4 times, miss next stitch, repeat from * to end of round. Join with slip stitch to 4th chain.

Round 19: Slip stitch into 3 chain space, 4 chain (count as 1st double treble), * [2 double treble, 3 chain, 2 double treble] in this space, 3 chain, miss 2 stitches, 5 double treble cluster round next stitch, 3 chain, 1 double treble in next stitch, 3 chain, miss next stitch, 5 double treble cluster round next stitch, 2 chain, 1 double treble into same space as cluster, miss 2 stitches, 8tr, miss 1 stitch, [4 chain, 1dc in next loop] 7 times, 4 chain, miss next stitch, 8tr, miss 2 stitches, 1 double treble in next space, 2 chain, 5 double treble cluster round next stitch, 3 chain, miss next stitch, 1 double treble in next stitch, 3 chain, 5 double treble cluster round next stitch, 3 chain, repeat from * to end of round. Join with slip stitch to 4th chain.

Round 20: Slip stitch into 3 chain space, 4 chain (count as 1st double treble), [2 double treble, 3 chain, 2 doube treble] in this space, 3 chain, miss 1 stitch, 1 double treble in next stitch, 3 chain, * [5 double treble cluster over cluster on previous round, 3 chain, 1 double treble in next stitch, 3 chain] twice, miss next stitch, 6 treble cluster over next 6 stitches, 3 chain, miss 1 stitch, [1tr, 1 chain, 1tr, 1 chain in next loop] 8 times, 2 chain, miss 1 stitch, 6 treble cluster over next 6 stitches, 3 chain, miss 1 stitch, 1 double treble in next stitch, 3 chain, [5 double treble cluster over cluster on previous round, 3 chain, 1 double treble in next stitch, 3 chain] twice, miss next stitch, repeat from * to end of round. Join with slip stitch to 4th chain.

Round 21: Slip stitch into 3 chain space, 3 chain (count as 1st treble), * [2tr, 3 chain, 2tr] into this space, 1 chain, [1tr, 1 chain] between next 2 stitches, [1tr in next space, 1 chain, 1tr in next stitch, 1 chain] 6 times, [1tr in next space, 1 chain] 17 times, [1tr in next stitch, 1 chain, 1tr in next space, 1 chain] 6 times, [1tr between next 2 stitches, 1 chain] repeat from * to end of round. Join with slip stitch to 3rd chain.

Round 22: Slip stitch into 3 chain space, 3 chain (count as 1st treble), * [3tr, 3 chain, 3tr] into this space, [2 chain, miss 2 stitches, 3tr] 18 times, miss 2 stitches, repeat from * to end of round, 2 chain. Join with slip stitch to 3rd chain.

Round 23: Slip stitch into 3 chain space, 3 chain (count as 1st treble), * [3tr, 3 chain, 3tr] into this space, 3tr in next 3tr, [2 chain, 3tr in next 3tr] to corner, 3tr, repeat from * to end of round. Join with slip stitch to 3rd chain.

Round 24: Slip stitch into 3 chain space, 3 chain (count as 1st treble) * [3tr, 3 chain, 3tr] into this space, 2 chain, miss 1st 3 stitches, [3tr in next 3tr, 2 chain] to last 6tr before corner, 3tr, 2 chain, miss 3tr, repeat from * to end of round. Join with slip stitch to 3rd chain.

Round 25: As round 23.
Round 26: As round 24.
Round 27: Slip stitch into 3 chain space, 3 chain (count as 1st treble), * [3tr, 3 chain, 3tr] into this space, [3tr in each tr, 2tr in each space to corner], repeat from * to end of round. Join with slip stitch to 3rd chain. Fasten off.

TO MAKE UP

Weave in all ends, lay work out flat and cover with a fine cloth and steam gently. Cut the backing fabric to 101cm long by 42cm wide.
Make a hem along each of the short edges by folding under 1.5cm then 4cm to the wrong side. Pin and tack hem, then topstitch. Remove tacking stitches and press.
Lay the crochet on a flat surface with the right side facing upwards and overlap them by 12cm so that the cover measures 39cm from fold to fold.
Pin the open sides together, tack and then sew the seams 1.5cm from the raw edges. Trim the seams and finish the raw edges with a zig zag stitch, if possible. Remove the tacking stitches and turn cushion cover right side out. Press.

TO FINISH

Hand stitch the crochet to the front of the fabric cover, carefully stitching around the edge of the filet square.

Patchwork throw

Motifs are characteristic of crochet: small and versatile, they take no time to make and can be picked up, put down, even forgotten about for ages and then started up again. At first glance this throw looks a little daunting to make, but it is a collection of simple six-sided motifs. Worked in single crochet in two colours, it gives a very effective 'spot' design. Take time when considering your combinations but don't be too prescriptive. Work as many motifs as you need and sew them together with a simple oversewn stitch to keep the throw flat. This throw works well in both contemporary and traditional interiors or as a useful accessory in the car.

Making the Patchwork throw

THROW SIZE
Approximately 159cm x 167cm, but measurements can be easily adjusted as required

MATERIALS
Rowan Cotton Glace or similar medium-weight glazed cotton yarn (see page 170) in 12 contrasting colours as follows:

Colour A: 7 x 50g balls in orange
Colour B: 7 x 50g balls in hot pink
Colour C: 7 x 50g balls in olive green
Colour D: 7 x 50g balls in dark green
Colour E: 7 x 50g balls in pale pink
Colour F: 7 x 50g balls in light blue
Colour G: 7 x 50g balls in lilac
Colour H: 7 x 50g balls in purple
Colour I: 7 x 50g balls in grey
Colour J: 7 x 50g balls in yellow
Colour K: 7 x 50g balls in plum
Colour L: 7 x 50g balls in fuchsia
Hook size 3.00mm
Large sewing needle

STITCH SIZE
Each hexagonal motif measures 10cm in diameter when worked in treble crochet over five rounds.

TECHNIQUES USED
Treble crochet and working in rounds.

For treble crochet: see page 16

For working in rounds: see page 22

TIPS
Tension: Don't worry about tension too much! Because these motifs are made in circles, you can work your stitches in rounds until it is the required size.

Working in rounds: When you work in rounds, you never have to turn the fabric. The right side is always facing you.

Marking the beginning of a round: Mark the beginning of each round to make it easier to keep your place.

Joining in a new yarn: Begin the last treble crochet in the usual way, but change to the new yarn when drawing the yarn through to the last loop of the stitch. Leave a long loose end of the old and new yarns to weave in later or work over the ends for several stitches before clipping them off.

Yarns: You can use up odd balls of yarn to make this throw – as it is made up of lots

of small motifs, mixed dye lots do not matter. End of line colours, often from the sale bin or oddments from your own stash, can make a great throw in the age-old tradition of patchwork.

METHOD

Hexagonal motif

Base ring: Leaving a long loose end and using first colour, chain 4, join length of chain into ring by working a slip stitch into 1st chain made.

Round 1: Chain 3 (counts as 1tr), 1tr into ring, [1 chain, 2tr into ring] 5 times, 1 chain, slip stitch to top of 3 chain. [6 spaces.]

Round 2: Slip stitch into next treble and into next chain, 3 chain (counts as 1tr), * 2tr **, work a V stitch of 1tr 1 chain 1tr into next space, repeat from * 4 times and from * to ** once, 1tr into last space, 1 chain, slip stitch to top of 3 chain. Change to second colour.

Round 3: Chain 3 (counts as 1tr), 1tr in each treble and 1 V stitch into each space all around, ending with a slip stitch to top of 3 chain. [6 groups of 6 trebles.]

Round 4: As round 3. [6 groups of 8 trebles.]

Round 5: As round 3. [6 groups of 10 trebles.]
Fasten off.

This completes one motif. Work the number of motifs required in combinations of any two colours of your choice. For the size of throw here 295 motifs are required.

TO FINISH

Weave any loose ends into the wrong side of the work. Lay the work out flat, then steam and press lightly.

Lay the motifs out flat alternating rows of 16 motifs and rows of 15 motifs.

Join together with strands of colored yarn with small, neat oversewn stitches.

Using the colour of your choice, rejoin the yarn and work a row of trebles around the edge of the throw, working a V stitch into each V stitch and working 2tr together where the motifs join to keep the throw flat.

Contemporary

Simple textures and freeform organic structures are the perfect foils to bold, modern décor. Add a new dimension by contrasting the handmade with the hard edged. The wood, glass, Perspex and ceramic of contemporary interiors are softened by silky cotton, whisper fine mohair, homely wool and sumptuous cashmere to create a contemporary update on classic homewares – the net curtain, the table runner, the comfortable cushions. A distinctive statement, especially when refined to simple black and white.

Spider's web curtain

A twist on a traditional lacy net curtain, this is worked in whisper fine mohair with a metallic shimmer. The drape is trimmed with random asymmetrical crochet motifs and then further decorated with sequins for a touch of glamour.

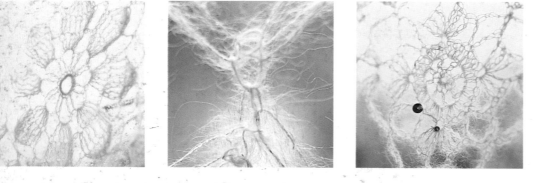

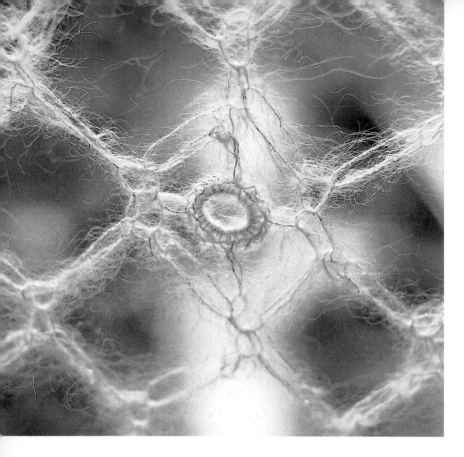

Making the Spider's web curtain

CURTAIN SIZE

Approximately 250cm x 120cm, but size can be easily adjusted as required

MATERIALS

5 x 25g balls Rowan Kidsilk Haze or similar 4-ply weight mohair yarn (see page 170)
Hook sizes 2.50mm and 5.00mm
Sequins

STITCH SIZE

This curtain has a tension of 5 stitches and 7 rows to 20cm measured over Solomon's Knot pattern using hook size 5.00mm.

TECHNIQUES USED

Solomon's Knot stitch

For Solomon's Knot: see page 21

TIPS

Tension: Don't worry about tension too much! Because this curtain is made in multiples, you can work extra stitches until the curtain is the required size.

Edge Solomon's Knot (ESK): These form the base "chain" and edges of the fabric and are only two-thirds the length of the Main Solomon's Knot.

Main Solomon's Knot (MSK): These form the main fabric and are a little longer than the Edge Solomon's Knot.

METHOD

Foundation 'chain': Using 5.00mm hook, chain 2, 1dc into 2nd chain from hook, work 52ESK and 1MSK.

Row 1: 1dc into dc between 3rd and 4th loops from hook, * 2MSK, miss 2 loops, 1dc into next dc, repeat from * to end.

Row 2: 2ESK, 1MSK, 1dc into dc between 4th and 5th loops from hook, * 2MSK, miss 2 loops, 1dc into next dc, repeat from * ending in top of ESK.

Repeat row 2 until work measures 250cm or required length.

Square motif

Base ring: Using 5.00mm hook, chain 4 and join length of chain into ring by working a slip stitch into 1st chain made.

Round 1: Work 8dc into ring, slip stitch to 1st dc.

Round 2: Chain 4, 1tr, * 1 chain, 1tr, repeat from * ending 1 chain, slip stitch into 3rd of 4 chain. [8 chain spaces.]

Round 3: Chain 3, 3tr into 1 chain space, * 1tr, 3tr into 1 chain space, repeat from * ending slip stitch into 3rd of 3 chain. [31 trebles.]

Round 4: Chain 9, 1 double treble into same place as slip stitch, * miss 3tr, 3 double treble 5 chain 3 double treble into next treble, miss 3tr, 1 double treble 5 chain 1 double treble into next treble, repeat from * ending slip stitch into 4th of 9 chain.

Round 5: Slip stitch to centre of 5 chain, 1dc into space, 7 chain, ** 3 double treble 5 chain 3 double treble into 5 chain space, 7 chain, dc into 5 chain space, 7 chain, repeat from ** ending slip stitch into 1st dc. Fasten off.

Star motif

Base ring: Using 5.00mm hook, chain 6 and join length of chain into ring by working a slip stitch into 1st chain made.

Round 1: Chain 1, [1dc into ring, 3 chain] 12 times, slip stitch to 1st dc.

Round 2: Slip stitch into each of next 2 chain, 1 chain, 1dc into same 3 chain arch, [3 chain, 1dc into next 3 chain arch] 11 times, 1 chain, 1 half treble into top of 1st dc.

Round 3: * chain 6, 1dc into next 3 chain arch **, chain 3, 1dc into next 3 chain arch, repeat from * 4 times and from * to ** once, chain 1, 1tr into half treble that closed previous round.

Round 4: * [5tr 2 chain 5tr] into next 6 chain arch, 1dc into next 3 chain arch, repeat from * 5 times ending last repeat in treble that closed previous round, slip stitch into next stitch. Fasten off.

Treble star motif

Base ring: Wind yarn 7 times round little finger to form a circle and using 5.00mm hook slip stitch into ring to secure.

Round 1: Chain 3, 3tr into circle, [9 chain, 4tr into ring] 5 times, 9 chain, slip stitch into top of 1st 3 chain.

Round 2: Slip stitch into 1st treble, * 1dc, [9tr 2 chain, 9tr] into next 9 chain loop, miss next 2tr, repeat from * 5 times, slip stitch into 1st dc. Turn.

Round 3: Slip stitch into each of 1st 4tr, * 5dc, 2dc into next 2 chain loop, 5dc, 2 chain, miss next 8tr, repeat from * 5 times, slip stitch to 1st dc. Fasten off.

Webbed star motif

Base ring: Using 5.00mm hook, chain 8 and join length of chain into ring by working a slip stitch into 1st chain made.

Round 1: [chain 14, 1dc into 7th chain from hook, 7 chain, 1dc into circle] 7 times, 14 chain, 1dc into 7th chain from hook, yarn round hook 6 times, insert hook into circle, yarn round hook and draw through a loop, [yarn round hook and draw through 1st 2 loops on hook] 6 times, yarn round hook and draw through remaining two loops on hook.

Round 2: * Chain 5, [1dc, 5 chain] 4 times into next 6 chain loop, 1dc into same loop, repeat from * 7 times. Fasten off.

Small circle motif

Base ring: Wind yarn 8 times round little finger to form a circle and using 2.50mm hook slip stitch into circle to secure.

Round 1: Chain 1, 20dc into ring, slip stitch to 1st dc. Fasten off.

Small flowers motif

Base ring: Wind yarn 8 times round little finger to form a circle and using 2.50mm hook slip stitch into circle to secure

Round 1: Chain 1, 20dc into ring, slip stitch to 1st dc.

Round 2: [Chain 3, 1dc into next dc, miss next dc] repeat all round. Fasten off.

Large round motif

Base ring: Using 5.00mm hook, work rounds 1 to 7 inclusive of motif given for String Stool (see pages 56–7).

Small round motif

Base ring: Using 2.50mm hook, chain 4 and join length of chain into ring by working a slip stitch into 1st chain made.

Round 1: 8dc into ring, slip stitch into 1st dc.

Round 2: Chain 4, 1 double treble into same place as slip stitch, [3 chain, 2 double treble into next dc] repeat all around ending 3 chain, slip stitch into 4th of 4 chain. Fasten off.

Six-petal flower motif

Base ring: Wind yarn 10 times round little finger to form a circle and using 2.50mm hook work 30dc into ring.

Round 1: 1dc into each dc, join with slip stitch to 1st dc.

Round 2: 1dc into next dc, * 12 chain, 5dc, repeat from * ending with 12 chain, 4dc, slip stitch into 1st dc.

Round 3: * Into next 12 chain loop work 2dc 2 half treble 9tr 2 half treble 2dc, miss 1dc, 3dc, repeat from * to end.

Round 4: * 17dc, miss 1dc, slip stitch into next dc, miss 1dc, repeat from * to end. Fasten off.

TO FINISH

Lay the work out flat and arrange the motifs at the bottom edge of the curtain as preferred. Attach lightly with the same yarn. Adorn with as many or as few sequins as you prefer.

Moulded wire mat

Worked in wire, crochet takes on a whole new appearance! This is a very distinctive piece to crochet. Pliable wire in in hues of blues, violets, bronze and turquoise are made into simple motifs in various sizes and assembled in a very free way to give a twist on the traditional 'Afghan' motif. They are attached and filled in with random chains of crochet, twisted and scrunched to create an unusual yet very decorative piece for the table with a very individual look.

Making the Moulded wire mat

MAT SIZE

Approximately 28cm x 36cm, but size can be easily adjusted as required

MATERIALS

Assorted reels of coloured artistic wire, 24 gauge (0.5mm) (available from most good craft or bead shops)
Hook size 4.50mm

STITCH SIZE

Each large circular motif measures 5cm in diameter when worked in double crochet.

TECHNIQUES USED

Double crochet and working in rounds.

For double crochet: see page 14

For working in rounds: see page 22

TIPS

Tension: Don't worry about tension too much! Because these motifs are made in circles, you can work your stitches in rounds until it is the required size.

Working in rounds: When you work in rounds, you never have to turn the fabric. The right side is always facing you.

METHOD

Large circular motif

Base ring: Wind wire 4 times round little finger to form a circle and using 4.50mm hook work 16dc into ring, slip stitch to 1st dc.

Next round: Chain 1, 1dc in same place as turning chain, * 2dc in next dc, repeat from * to end. Join with slip stitch to chain. Fasten off leaving 15cm length of wire to join motifs.

Small circular motifs

Work as Large circular motif but fasten off after 16dc have been worked.

TO FINISH

Sketch a diagram of where you want each motif to be. Using any colour wire and any long ends, join the motifs to form the outer edge. Refer to your diagram to make sure they are in the correct position. Join the motifs with a few chain stitches, cut the wire and fasten off by pushing the ends through the work. Fill in by crocheting small lengths of chain with a long piece of wire either end and use these as links – pushing the wires through the edges of the circles. Either ensure work is lying flat or scrunch as you go for more decorative effect.

Round rose cushion

A rose by any other name may not smell as sweet, but this crochet cushion is certainly a heavenly project. An intriguing change from the conventional square cushion shape, this cushion cover is worked in rounds to form petal shapes and so can be made to fit any size cushion pad. This project is saved from being too twee by the contemporary black and white colourway. It could be given a modern country look, however, if made in string with a floral print fabric underneath.

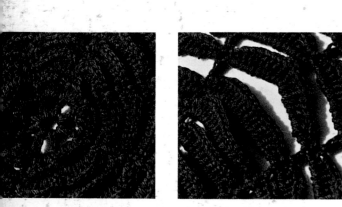

Making the Round rose cushion

CUSHION SIZE
Approximately 38cm in diameter, but size can be easily adjusted as required

MATERIALS
4 x 50g balls Rowan Classic Cashwool or similar double-knitting weight yarn (see page 170)
Hook size 3.00mm
Circular cushion pad, 38cm in diameter

STITCH SIZE
This cushion has a tension of 5 rounds to 8.5cm measured over pattern using a 3.00mm hook, but working to an exact tension is not essential (see Tips).

TECHNIQUES USED
Double, treble, half treble and double treble crochet and working in rounds

For double crochet: see page 14

For treble crochet: see page 16

For half treble crochet: see page 18

For double treble crochet: see page 19

For working in rounds: see page 22

TIPS
Tension: Don't worry about tension too much! Because this cushion cover is made in circles, you can work your stitches in rounds until the cover has reached the required size.

Working in rounds: When you work in rounds, you never have to turn the fabric. The right side is always facing you.

Marking the beginning of a round: Mark the beginning of each round to make it easier to keep your place.

Making a round cushion pad: Customise a square cushion pad by first chalking a 38cm circle on the pad. Then take each corner in turn, shake the stuffing to the middle, fold down the empty corners and stitch through both layers along the chalked line.

METHOD
Front and Back (make 2)
Base ring: Chain 6 and join length of chain into ring by working a slip stitch into 1st chain made.

Round 1: 5 chain, [1tr, 2 chain] 7 times into ring, slip stitch to 3rd of 5 chain. [8 spaces.]

Round 2: * 1dc, 1 half treble 3tr 1 half treble 1dc in space, repeat from * in each space to end, slip stitch to 1st dc. [8 petals.]

Round 3: * 4 chain, 1dc between next 2 petals, repeat from * to end.

Round 4: * 1dc 1 half treble 5tr 1 half treble 1dc in loop, repeat from * in each loop to end, slip stitch to 1st dc.

Round 5: * 6 chain, 1dc between next 2 petals, repeat from * to end.

Round 6: * 1dc 1 half treble 7tr 1 half treble 1dc in loop, repeat from * in each loop to end, slip stitch to 1st dc.

Round 7: * 8 chain, 1dc between next 2 petals, repeat from * to end.

Round 8: * 1dc 1 half treble 9tr 1 half treble 1dc in loop, repeat from * in each loop to end, slip stitch to 1st dc.

Round 9: * 10 chain, 1dc between next 2 petals, repeat from * to end.

Round 10: * 1dc 1 half treble 11tr 1 half treble 1dc in loop, repeat from * in each loop to end, slip stitch to 1st dc.

Round 11: * 12 chain, 1dc between next 2 petals, repeat from * to end.

Round 12: * 1dc 1 half treble 13tr 1 half treble 1dc in loop, repeat from * in each loop to end, slip stitch to 1st dc.

Round 13: * 14 chain, 1dc between next 2 petals, repeat from * to end.

Round 14: * 1dc 1 half treble 15tr 1 half treble 1dc in loop, repeat from * in each loop to end, slip stitch to 1st dc.

Round 15: * 16 chain, 1dc between next 2 petals, repeat from * to end.

Round 16: * 1dc 1 half treble 17tr 1 half treble 1dc in loop, repeat from * in each loop to end, slip stitch to 1st dc.

Round 17: * 9 chain, 1dc behind centre treble on next petal, 9 chain, 1dc between next 2 petals, repeat from * to end.

Round 18: * 1dc 1 half treble 9tr 1 half treble 1dc in loop, repeat from * in each 9 chain loop to end, slip stitch to 1st dc.

Round 19: * 10 chain, 1dc between next 2 petals, repeat from * to end.

Round 20: * 1dc 1 half treble 10tr 1 half treble 1dc in loop, repeat from * in each loop to end, slip stitch to 1st dc.

Round 21: * 11 chain, 1dc between next 2 petals, repeat from * to end.

Round 22: * 1dc 1 half treble 11tr 1 half treble 1dc in loop, repeat from * in each loop to end, slip stitch to 1st dc.

Round 23: * 12 chain, 1dc between next 2 petals, repeat from * to end.

Round 24: * 1dc 1 half treble 12tr 1 half treble 1dc in loop, repeat from * in each loop to end, slip stitch to 1st dc.

Round 25: 4 chain, * miss 1dc and 1 half

treble, 12tr, miss 1 half treble and 1dc, 1 double treble between petals, repeat from * to end, slip stitch to top of 4 chain.
Round 26: Chain 3, tr to end. Fasten off.

TO FINISH
Weave any loose ends into the wrong side of the work. Lay the work out flat, then steam and press lightly.

Place the pieces together with wrong sides facing and pin. Oversew the edge until the opening is just large enough to enclose the cushion pad.

Insert the cushion pad and finish sewing the edge to close. Fasten off and weave in the yarn end.

Appliqué flower cushion

This is a very easy yet effective home accessory project. Simple crochet motifs are sewn onto a knitted cushion cover for contrast. Make in self-colour or contrast colour and decorate with French knots or beads. Alternatively make in more colourful yarns and textures and combine with print or pattern cushion covers to compliment a vintage look.

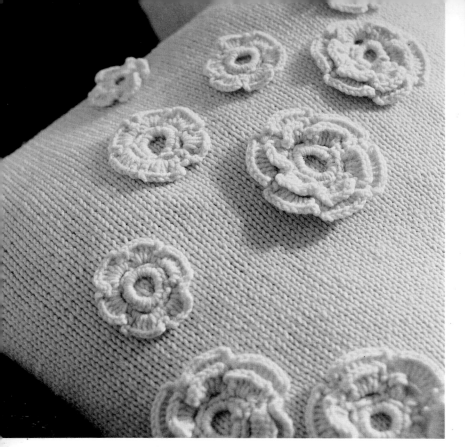

Making the Appliqué flower cushion

CUSHION SIZE

Small, medium and large flowers can be appliquéd onto the cushion of your choice

MATERIALS

1 x 50g ball Jaeger DK Merino or a similar double-knitting weight yarn (see page 170) will make 4 large, 4 medium and 4 small flowers

Hook sizes 2.00mm and 3.00mm

STITCH SIZE

The motifs should measure 7.5cm for the large size, 6.5cm for the medium size and 5cm for the small size, but working to an exact tension is not essential (see Tips).

TECHNIQUES USED

Double crochet, treble crochet and working in rounds.

| For double crochet: see page 14 |
| For treble crochet: see page 16 |
| For working in rounds: see page 22 |

TIPS

Tension: Don't worry about tension too much! Because these flower motifs are made in circles, you can work your stitches in rounds until it is the required size.

Working in rounds: When you work in rounds, you never have to turn the fabric. The right side is always facing you.

METHOD

Large rose

Base ring: Using a hook size 3.00mm, chain 12 and join length of chain into ring by working a slip stitch into 1st chain made.

Round 1 (right side): Chain 1, work 18dc into ring, join with a slip stitch into 1st dc.

Round 2: Chain 1, 1dc into same stitch as 1 chain, 3ch, miss 2 stitches [1dc, 3ch, miss 2 stitches] 5 times, slip stitch to 1st dc.

Round 3: Chain 1, [in next 3 chain loop work a petal of 1dc, 3ch, 5tr, 3ch, 1dc] 6 times, slip stitch to 1st dc.

Round 4: Chain 1, [1dc between 2dc, 5 chain behind petal of Round 3] 6 times, slip stitch to 1st dc.

Round 5: Chain 1, [in next 5 chain loop work a petal of 1dc, 3ch, 7tr, 3ch, 1dc] 6

times, slip stitch to 1st dc.
Fasten off leaving long end.

Medium rose
Work as given for Large rose, working Rounds 1 to 3 inclusive.

Small rose
Using hook size 2.0mm, work as given for Medium rose.

TO FINISH
Weave any loose ends into the wrong side of the work.
Pin flowers randomly on to your chosen cushion cover and then sew into position. If desired, further embellish the pillow with a beads or French knots.
French knot embroidery: To make a French knot, bring the thread out at the required position, hold the thread down where it emerges with the left thumb and encircle the thread twice with the needle. Still holding the thread firmly with your thumb, twist the needle back to the starting point and insert it close to where the thread first emerged (not in the exact place or it will simply pull back through). Pull the needle through to the back, leaving a small knot on the surface, or pass on to the position of the next stitch.

Making a knitted pillow

PILLOW SIZE
Pillow cover is approximately 40cm x 40cm

MATERIALS
6 x 50g balls Jaeger Extra Fine Merino or a similar double-knitting weight yarn (see page 170)
1 pair each of 3.25mm and 4mm knitting needles
Sewing needle
40cm x 40cm cushion pad
5 buttons, approximately 2cm in diameter

STITCH SIZE
22 stitches and 32 rows to 10cm over stockinette stitch on 4mm needles.

METHOD
Back
With 4mm needles, cast on 90 stitches and work 40cm in stocking stitch – knit 1 row, purl 1 row alternately – finishing with a purl row (wrong side).
Button band
Starting with a knit row, work 10 rows in stocking stitch.
Next row (right side): Change to 3.25mm needles, purl to end.
Next row (wrong side): Change to 4mm needles, purl to end.
Starting with a knit row work a further 9 rows in stocking stitch. Cast off.

Front
With 4mm needles, cast on 90 stitches and work 40cm in stocking stitch – knit 1 row, purl 1 row alternately – finishing with a purl row (wrong side).

Buttonhole band
Starting with a knit row, work 4 rows in stocking stitch.
Row 5 (buttonhole): Knit 8 stitches, cast off next 3 stitches, [knit until 15 stitches on right-hand needle after last cast off, cast off next 3 stitches] 4 times, knit to end.
Row 6: Purl across row, casting on 3 stitches over those cast off in previous row.
Work 4 more rows in stocking stitch, finishing with a purl row.
Next row (right side): Change to 3.25mm needles, purl to end.
Next row (wrong side): Change to 4mm needles, purl to end.
Starting with a knit row work a further 3 rows in stocking stitch.
Repeat rows 5 and 6.
Work a further 4 rows in stocking stitch.
Cast off.

TO FINISH
Weave any loose ends into the wrong side of the work. Lay the pieces out flat, then steam and press lightly.
Pin back and front pieces with right sides together. Use a small neat backstitch to join three sides, leaving the buttonhole band open.
Next fold the button bands in half along the purl stitch row and sew to the inside. Turn cushion cover right side out and sew on the buttons to correspond with the buttonholes.
Insert the cushion pad and button up.

Round floor rug

A playful twist on traditional crochet, a doilly for the floor, this rug is perfect for adding a little bit of warmth, texture and colour to any interior. Quick to make too, this project can be created over a weekend to add instant, practical glamour. Made in fat yarn worked on a small hook to give a felted appearance, this rug could just as easily be made in multi ends of various yarns for a different look, just take care to catch all the ends with the hook!

Making the Round floor rug

RUG SIZE

Approximately 92cm in diameter, but size can be easily adjusted as required

MATERIALS

7 x 100g balls Rowan Big Wool or similar fat wool yarn (see page 170)
Hook size 7.00mm

STITCH SIZE

Working to an exact tension is not essential (see Tips).

TECHNIQUES USED

Double crochet, treble crochet and working in rounds

For double crochet: see page 14

For treble crochet: see page 16

For working in rounds: see page 22

TIPS

Tension: Don't worry about tension too much! Because this rug is made in circles, you can work your stitches in rounds until it is the required size.

Working in rounds: When you work in rounds, you never have to turn the fabric. The right side is always facing you.

Marking the beginning of a round: Mark the beginning of each round to make it easier to keep your place.

METHOD

Base ring: Chain 9 and join length of chain into ring by working a slip stitch into 1st chain made.

Round 1: Chain 3, 17tr into ring, slip stitch into top of 3 chain.

Round 2: Chain 3, 1tr 2 chain 2tr into same stitch as 3 chain, * 1 chain, miss 2tr, 2tr 2 chain 2tr into next tr, repeat from * all round, ending with 1 chain, miss 2tr, slip stitch into top of 3 chain.

Round 3: Slip stitch into 1tr and into space, 3 chain, 1tr 2 chain 2tr into same space as slip stitch, * 1 chain 1tr into next space, 1 chain 2tr 2 chain 2tr into next space, repeat from * all round, ending with 1 chain 1tr into space, 1 chain, slip stitch into top of 3 chain.

Round 4: Slip stitch into 1tr and into space, 3 chain, 1tr 2 chain 2tr into same space as slip stitch, * 1 chain 1tr into next space, 2 chain 1tr into next space, 1 chain 2tr 2

chain 2tr into next space, repeat from * all round, ending with 1 chain 1tr into next space, 2 chain 1tr into next space, 1 chain slip stitch into top of 3 chain.

Round 5: Slip stitch into 1tr and into space, 3 chain, 1tr 2 chain 2tr into space, * 1 chain 1tr into next space, 1 chain 5tr into next space, 1 chain 1tr into next space, 1 chain 2tr 2 chain 2tr into next space, repeat from * all round, ending with 1 chain 1tr into space, 1 chain 5tr into next space, 1 chain 1tr into next space, 1 chain, slip stitch into top of 3 chain.

Round 6: Slip stitch into 1tr and into space, 3 chain, 1tr 2 chain 2tr into space, * 1 chain 1tr into next space, 1 chain, miss 1 space, 2tr into next tr, 3tr, 2tr into next tr, 1 chain, miss 1 space, 1tr into next space, 1 chain 2tr 2 chain 2tr into next space, repeat from * all round, ending with 1 chain 1tr into next space, 1 chain, miss 1 space, 2tr into next treble, 3tr, 2tr into next tr, 1 chain, miss 1 space, 1tr into next space, 1 chain, slip stitch into top of 3 chain.

Round 7: Work as Round 6, working 2tr into each tr, 1tr into each of the next 5tr, 2tr Into tr.

Continue working the extra trebles until there are 21tr in each group of trebles.

Round 14: Slip stitch into tr, 1dc into space, * 5 chain, miss 1 space, 3tr into next space, 2 chain, miss 1tr, 19tr, 2 chain, 3tr into next space, 5 chain, miss 1 space, 1dc, repeat from * all round, finish 5 chain, slip stitch into 1st dc.

Round 15: Slip stitch into 2 chain, 1dc into space, * 5 chain, 3tr into next space, 2 chain, miss 1tr, 17tr, 2 chain, 3tr into next space, [5 chain, 1dc] into each of next 2 spaces, repeat from * all round, finish 5 chain, slip stitch into 1st dc.

Continue as last round, working 2tr less in each group of tr and [5 chain, 1dc] into extra space on each round, until 7 stitches remain.

Next round: Slip stitch into 2 chain, 1dc into space, * 5 chain, 3tr into next space, 2 chain, miss 1tr, leaving last loop of each tr on hook, 1tr into each of next 5tr, draw yarn through remaining stitches, 2 chain, 3tr into space, [5 chain, 1dc] into each of next 8 spaces, repeat from * all round, ending with [5 chain, 1dc] into each of next 7 spaces, 5 chain, slip stitch into 1st dc.

Edging

3dc, 5 chain, slip stitch into 5th chain from hook (the picot) 3dc into space, * 3dc, 2dc into space, 1 picot, 2dc into next space, 3dc, [3dc 1 picot 3dc] into each of next 9 spaces, repeat from * all round, join with slip stitch. Fasten off.

TO FINISH

Weave any loose ends into the wrong side of the work. Lay the work out flat, then steam and press lightly.

Organic table runner

Simply draw freehand a very amoeba-like shape onto a piece of graph paper, roughly the width and length preferred to fit your table or sideboard. Work a collection of random motifs – some half motifs and some with extensions grafted on to make irregular shapes. Pin the finished motifs haphazardly onto your chosen shape and link them with chains, whilst still pinned onto the paper, and in turn add extra little bits to these linking chains to create a completely unique, one-off piece of creative crochet. This runner is made in mercerised cotton and is trimmed with jet beads, perfect for the modern coffee table or retro sideboard.

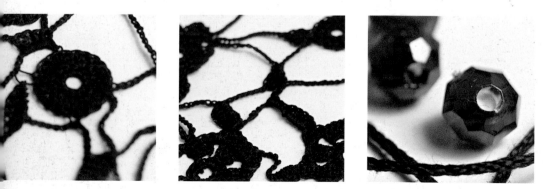

Making the Organic table runner

RUNNER SIZE

Approximately 92cm x 28cm, but size can be easily adjusted as required

MATERIALS

Approximately 50g Yeomans Cotton Cannele or similar 4-ply mercerised cotton yarn (see page 170)

Hook size 3.00mm

Approximately 25 beads

STITCH SIZE

Working to an exact tension is not essential (see Tips).

TECHNIQUES USED

Double, treble and half treble crochet and working in rounds.

| For double crochet: see page 14 |
| For treble crochet: see page 16 |
| For half treble crochet: see page 18 |
| For working in rounds: see page 22 |

TIPS

Tension: Don't worry about tension too much! If your motifs ends up a bit bigger or smaller than the size given here, just add more motifs to achieve the required size.

METHOD

Sketch out required shape for your design onto squared paper to make a template. Make as many of the following as required:

Rosette A

Base ring: Chain 7, join with slip stitch.

Round 1: Chain 1, 12dc into ring, join with slip stitch into 1st dc, 3 chain.

Round 2: 1tr into next stitch, * 3 chain, 2tr, repeat from * 4 times, 3 chain, join with slip stitch to top of 3 chain.

Rosette B

Base ring: Chain 6, join with slip stitch.

Round 1: Chain 1, 16dc into ring, slip stitch to 1st dc.

Round 2: Chain 6, miss 2 stitches, * 1tr, 3 chain, miss 1 stitch, repeat from * 6 times, slip stitch to 3rd chain of 6 chain.

Round 3: Chain 1, * 1dc 1 half treble 5tr 1 half treble 1dc in 3 chain space, repeat from * 7 times, slip stitch to 1st dc.

Rosette C

Base ring: Work 10 chain, join with slip stitch.
Round 1: 24dc into ring, slip stitch into 1st dc.
Round 2: * 6 chain, miss 2dc, 1dc, repeat from * 7 times, slip stitch into 1st chain.
Round 3: * 8dc into next 6 chain space, repeat from * 7 times, slip stitch into 1st dc.

Rosette D

Base ring: Work 10 chain, join with slip stitch.
Round 1: 24 half treble into ring, slip stitch into 1st half treble.

Rosette E

Base ring: Work 6 chain, join with slip stitch.
Row 1: Chain 1, 18dc into ring, 6 chain. Turn.
Row 2: Miss 2 stitches, * 1tr, 3 chain, miss 1 stitch, repeat from * 3 times. Turn.
Row 3: Chain 1, 1dc 1 half treble 5tr 1 half treble 1dc in 3 chain space, repeat from * 3 times.

TO FINISH

Pin each motif onto the paper template in the position required. (In the sample photographed, the spaces between each motif are approximately 4cm.)
Onto the paper template, draw as many linking chains between the motifs as preferred.
Crochet the linking chains following the pencil lines, but keep the motifs attached to the template. Join to the first motif with a slip stitch, make a chain to the next motif and join to that motif with a slip stitch.
Insert a groups of trebles at each intersection point of two or more chains.
Weave in any yarn ends.
Attach beads at random as preferred.

Heirloom

These exquisite vintage-inspired pieces will give a special welcome to any new baby, be cherished enough to be passed down to siblings and then be treasured as keepsakes once baby has grown up. In a colour palette of muted pastel shades and classic creams, this is a collection of adorable items for the nursery bottom drawer ranging from throws and shawl, to a bonnet and bootees. Made in basic double and treble crochet, these projects are simply embellished with small motifs and given added interest with easy decorative edgings.

Daisy-chain cot blanket

A beautiful gift to make for a new baby's cot or stroller. This blanket is crocheted in a wool cotton yarn, which feels wonderfully smooth and is very practical – it will keep baby snug in winter and comfortably cool during the warmer months. The crochet stitch used here imitates a woven fabric and gives an interesting texture to such a simple project. The tiny crocheted flowers and the picot stitch trim pick out the colours of the vintage fabric, which is used to line the blanket. You could use patches of any favourite material pieced together to make it more individual. If you're decorating a baby's room, this would be a lovely project to coordinate with the other nursery furnishings.

Making the Daisy-chain cot blanket

THROW SIZE
Approximately 127cm x 90cm

MATERIALS
Rowan Wool Cotton or a similar medium-weight cotton yarn (see page 170) in six colours:

Colour A: 18 x 50g balls in violet
Colour B: 2 x 50g balls in yellow
Colour C: 1 x 50g ball in camel
Colour D: 1 x 50g ball in russet
Colour E: 1 x 50g ball in green
Colour F: 1 x 50g ball in purple
Hook sizes 4.00mm and 3.50mm
Approximately 132cm x 95cm light-weight fabric, such as cotton, for backing
Large and fine sewing needles
Sewing thread

STITCH SIZE
This blanket has a tension of 22 stitches and 10 rows to 10cm measured over pattern of 1dc 1 chain.

TECHNIQUES USED
Double and treble crochet and picot edging (see pattern).

For double crochet: see page 14

For treble crochet: see page 16

METHOD
Foundation chain: Leaving a long loose end and using a hook size 4.00mm, chain 184.
Row 1: Work 1dc into 4th chain from hook, * 1 chain, miss 1 chain, 1dc into next chain, repeat from * to end. Turn.

Row 2: Chain 2 to count as 1st dc and 1st 1 chain space, miss 1st dc and work 1dc into 1st 1 chain space, * 1 chain, miss next dc, 1dc into next 1 chain space, repeat from * to end working last dc into chain space at edge. Turn.
Repeat row 2 until work measures 115cm from foundation chain edge. Fasten off.

Picot edging
For a detailed finish, work a simple picot-stitch edging all around the throw. Begin by joining a contrast yarn to a corner of the throw with a slip stitch then work the edging as follow:
Using hook size 3.50mm, work 1 row dc all round stitch for stitch and row for row. Work 3dc into each corner and join with

slip stitch to 1st stitch.

Now work a triple picot edging as follows:
2 chain, * 5dc, [3 chain, slip stitch into 3rd
chain from hook] 3 times, slip stitch into
top of last dc made.

Repeat from * all the way round.

In order to get a picot on each corner,
you may have to adjust the number of
dc between the picots at the end of a row.

Fasten off.

Weave any loose ends into the work.

Flowers (make 24)

Foundation chain: Using hook size
3.50mm and contrast colour, chain 2.

Row 1: 4dc into 2nd chain from hook,
slip stitch into 1st dc.

Row 2: 3 chain, work 3tr 3ch and 1 slip
stitch into same place as join, (1 slip stitch 3
chain 3tr 3 chain 1 slip stitch into next
stitch) 3 times. [4 petals.]

Work 1 slip stitch in joining stitch, 8 chain,
turn and starting with 2nd chain from
hook, slip stitch back along chain towards
the flower.

Fasten off leaving a long thread, which can
be used to attach flower.

Make 24 or as many flowers as required, in
different contrast colours.

TO FINISH

Weave any loose ends into the work.

Lay the work out flat, then steam and press
lightly. If necessary, pin out the work to
keep the corners square.

Place the flowers all around the edges of
the blanket, approximately 5cm in from the
outer edge.

Pin and then sew each flower into position
very firmly, taking care to remove all pins.

Cut the fabric to size of the blanket, adding
a hem allowance of 2.5cmm all the way
around. Pin and tack the fabric into
position, turning under 2.5cm at each edge,
smoothing as you go, and then sew neatly
with oversewn stitches. Remove any pins.

Lightly steam and press once more.

Nursery bear or bunny

Perfect for the nursery shelf, these little fellows sit and dangle their legs over the edge in a very relaxed manner. Whether a bear or a bunny, they are made in glazed cotton using basic double crochet. The head is worked in one piece to minimise the fiddly bits and too much sewing up. The bottom and feet are stuffed with beanbag filling to provide weight and help the toy stay put. The face is embroidered very simply and there are two sets of ears to choose from to make either bear or bunny. Bunny, of course, will require a pompom tail!

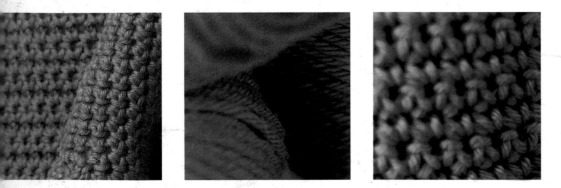

Making the Nursery bear or bunny

TOY SIZE

Approximately 40cm long measured from
foot to top of ear

MATERIALS

3 x 50g balls Rowan Cotton Glace
or similar medium-weight cotton yarn
(see page 170)
Hook size 2.50mm
½m fine satin ribbon, 3mm wide
Stuffing
Beanbag beads
Scraps of coloured yarn, for embroidery

STITCH SIZE

This bear or bunny has a tension of 20
stitches and 20 rows to 10cm measured
over double crochet

TECHNIQUES USED

Double crochet and working in rounds

For double crochet: see page 14

For working in rounds: see page 22

TIPS

Working in rounds: When you work in
rounds, you never have to turn the fabric.
The right side is always facing you.
Marking the beginning of a round:
Mark the beginning of each round to make
it easier to keep your place.

METHOD

Head (worked in one piece)
Foundation chain: Chain 17.
Row 1: 1dc in 2nd chain from hook,
1dc in every following chain, 1 chain.

Turn. [16 stitches.]
Row 2: 2dc in 1st dc, 5dc, 2dc in next dc,
2dc, 2dc in next dc, 5dc, 2dc in last dc, 1
chain. Turn. [20 stitches.]
Row 3: 2dc in 1st dc, 7dc, 2dc in next dc,
2dc, 2dc in next dc, 7dc, 2dc in last dc, 1
chain. Turn. [24 stitches.]
Work 4 rows straight in dc.
Next row: 9dc, miss 1dc, 4dc, miss 1dc, dc
to end, 1 chain. Turn.
Next row: 8dc, miss 1sc, 4dc, miss 1dc, dc
to end, 1 chain. Turn. [20 stitches.]
Work 26 rows without shaping.
Next row: 1dc in 1st dc, miss 1dc, 6dc,
miss 1dc, 2dc, miss 1dc, 6dc, miss 1dc, 1dc
in last dc. [16 stitches.]
Work 1 row straight in dc.
Fasten off.

Body (worked in one piece)

Foundation chain: Chain 59.

Row 1: 1dc in 2nd chain from hook, 1dc in every chain to end, 1 chain. Turn. [58dc.]

Row 2 and every alternate row: Dc to end, 1 chain. Turn.

Row 3: 19dc, dc 2 together, 16dc, dc 2 together, 19dc, 1 chain. Turn. [56dc.]

Row 5: 18dc, dc 2 together, 16dc, dc 2 together, 18dc. [54dc.]

Continue decreasing as set at each end of alternate rows until 32dc remain.

Work 2 rows straight.

Fasten off.

Body base

Foundation chain: Chain 4, join with slip stitch to form ring.

Round 1: Chain 1, 8dc into ring, join with slip stitch to 1st stitch.

Round 2: Chain 1, 2dc in each stitch to end, join with slip stitch. [16 stitches.]

Round 3: Chain 1 [2dc in next stitch, 1dc], repeat to end, join with slip stitch. [24 stitches.]

Round 4: Chain 1, [2dc, 2dc in next stitch] repeat to end, join with slip stitch. [32 stitches.]

Round 5: Chain 1, [2dc in next stitch, 3dc] repeat to end, join with slip stitch. [40 stitches.]

Continue increasing 8 stitches on every round until base measures 8cm in diameter. Fasten off.

Arms (make two)

Foundation chain: Chain 12, join with slip stitch to form ring.

Next round: 1dc in each chain. [12 stitches.]

Then work in spirals with 1dc in every dc until work measures 8cm. [Use a coloured thread to mark the end of the round.]

Next round: Work 2dc in next dc, 5dc, 2dc in next dc, 5dc. [14 stitches.]

Work 5 more rounds.

Turn and work as follows on 1st 7dc.

Next row: Chain 1, 7dc.

Now increase 1 stitch at each end of next and following 3rd row. [11 stitches.]

Work 2 rows straight.

Decrease 1 stitch at each end of next and following 2 rows. Fasten off.

Rejoin yarn to remaining 7dc and work to match.

Legs (make two)

The foot is worked first, sewn up and then the leg is worked last.

Foundation chain: Chain 29.

Row 1: 1dc in 2nd chain from hook, 1dc in each chain to end. Turn each row with 1 chain. [28 stitches.]

Increase 1 stitch at each end of next 2 rows. [32 stitches.]

Work 1 row dc.

Next row: Dc 2 together, dc to last 2 stitches, dc 2 together.

Repeat last row 5 times more. [20 stitches.] Fasten off.

Fold in half. Sew up sole of foot, round toe and the first 2dc either side of top.

Rejoin yarn to top of foot and working in spirals [18 stitches] dc from top of foot until leg measures 11cm.

Fasten off.

Bear ears (make two)

Foundation chain: Chain 7.

Row 1: 2dc in 2nd chain from hook, dc to last chain, 2dc in last chain.

Turn each row with 1 chain.

Next row: 2dc in 1st stitch, dc to last stitch, 2dc in last stitch.

Work 1 row dc.

Next row: 2dc in 1st stitch, dc to last stitch, 2dc in last stitch.

Work 2 rows dc.

Next row: Dc 2 together, dc to last 2 stitches, dc 2 together.

Work 1 row dc.

Repeat last 2 rows once more.

Fasten off.

Bunny ears (make two)

Foundation chain: Chain 9.

Row 1: 1dc into 2nd chain from hook, 1dc in each chain to end. [8 stitches.]

Turning each row with 1 chain, work 3 rows dc.

Next row: 2dc into 1st stitch, dc to last stitch, 2dc in last stitch.

Work 11 rows dc.

Next row: Dc 2 together, dc to last 2 stitches, dc 2 together.

Work 1 row dc.

Repeat last 2 rows until 4 stitches remain.

Fasten off.

Bunny tail

Cut out two circles of card, approximately 3cm in diameter and cut identical holes in the centre of each.

Hold the two circles together and with the yarn wind around the card circles. Work as many layers as you can before the centre hole disappears.

Using sharp scissors, slip one of the blades between the two outer layers of card and cut around the circumference of the circle.

Slip a length of yarn between the two layers and around the centre of what will

become the pompom, pull tight and knot the yarn.

Cut away the card, shake, fluff up and trim to shape.

Attach the pompom to the bottom of the bunny.

TO FINISH

For the head, fold in half and join the side seams. Stuff firmly with the stuffing.

For the arms, join the seam around each hand and stuff firmly with the stuffing.

For the legs, pour beanbag beads into each foot and then stuff firmly with the stuffing.

For the body, fold in half and join the seam down the centre back.

Attach the head to body at the neck. Pour beanbag beads into the base of the body and stuff the remaing body with the stuffing.

Attach the base to the body.

Sew the legs and arms into position on the body as shown.

Attach the ears to the head and embroider the face as shown.

Wrap a short length of ribbon around the bear's or bunny's neck and tie into a bow.

Sunday-best cardigan

The quintessential little baby cardigan never goes out of fashion as it is perfect for special occasions, such as a first outing or Christening. This is a good basic cardigan pattern which can be embellished to suit your own taste. Here it is edged in shiny satin ribbon that contrasts beautifully with the matt glazed cotton yarn. It is decorated with flowers crocheted in the same yarn and finished with pretty mother-of-pearl buttons, but it could just as easily be trimmed with bows or crocheted rosebuds.

Making the Sunday-best cardigan

CARDIGAN SIZE

To fit age (months):	0–3	3–6	6–9
Chest:	41cm	43.5cm	46cm
Actual chest:	50cm	55cm	60cm
Length:	24.5cm	29.5cm	34.5cm
Sleeve length:	15cm	19cm	21cm

MATERIALS

4 (5: 5) x 50g balls Rowan Cotton Glace or similar medium-weight cotton yarn (see page 170)

Hook sizes 2.50mm and 3.00mm

Approximately 12 (14: 15)m fine satin ribbon, 3mm wide

5 small buttons, 1.5cm in diameter

Sewing needle

STITCH SIZE

This cardigan has a tension of 20 stitches and 11 rows to 10cm measured over treble crochet using hook size 3.00mm.

TECHNIQUES USED

Treble crochet, simple shaping and picot edging (see pattern)

For treble crochet: see page 16

TIPS

Tension: Make a sample swatch of crochet to test your stitch size. If you are getting more than 20tr to 10cm, try a larger hook size; less the 20tr to 10cm, a smaller hook size. Don't worry too much about the number of rows to 10cm as you can easily adjust the length by adding rows.

METHOD

Back

Foundation chain: Using a hook size 3.0mm, chain 53 (58: 63).

Foundation row: 1tr in 4th chain from hook, tr to end. Turn. [50 (55: 60) stitches.]

Row 1: 3 chain to count as 1st tr, tr to end. Turn.

Repeat row 1 until work measures 13 (16.5: 19.5)cm. Turn.

Do not work 3 chain.

Shape armhole: Slip stitch over 1st 5 stitches of next row, 3 chain, tr to last 5 stitches. Turn. [40 (45: 50) stitches.] Continue working in tr without shaping until armhole measures 11.5 (13: 15)cm.

Shape shoulders and back neck: Tr across 1st 12 (14: 15) tr, dc across next 16 (17: 20) tr, 3 chain, tr across remaining 12 (14: 15) tr. Fasten off.

Left Front
Foundation chain: Chain 28 (31: 33).
Foundation row: As foundation row given for Back. [25 (28: 30) stitches.]
Row 1: As row 1 given for Back.
Repeat row 1 until work matches Back to armhole shaping.
Shape armhole: Slip stitch across 1st 5 stitches, 3 chain, tr to end. Turn. [20 (23: 25) stitches.]
Continue working in tr without shaping until armhole measures 7.5 (9: 11)cm finishing at armhole edge.
Shape neck: tr to last 5 stitches. Turn. [15 (18: 20) stitches.]
Decrease 1 stitch at neck edge of next 3 (4: 5) rows. [12 (14: 15) stitches.]
Work to match Back to shoulder. Fasten off.

Right Front
Work to match Left Front reversing shaping.

Sleeves (make 2)
Foundation chain: Chain 35 (39: 41).
Foundation row: As foundation row given for Back. [32 (36: 38) stitches.]
Work 3 rows tr.
Now increase 1 stitch at each end of next and every alternate row until 46 (52: 58) tr.
Continue without shaping until work measures 15 (19: 21)cm from start.
Mark both ends of last row.
Work 2 more rows of tr. Fasten off.

TO FINISH
Weave any loose ends into the work.
Lay the work out flat, then steam and

press lightly.
Join the shoulder seams. Sew the sleeve seams. The 2 last rows are stitched along the armhole shaping.
Sew side and sleeve seams.

Edging
Using hook size 2.50mm and ribbon, with right side of work facing and starting at centre back neck, work edging as follows:
* 1 slip stitch into 1st stitch, 3 chain, 1 slip stitch into same stitch, 1 slip stitch over 3 stitches, repeat from * all round edge of jacket.
Fasten off.

Flowers (make 4–6)
Foundation chain: Using hook size 3.00mm, chain 2.
Row 1: 4dc into 2nd chain from hook, slip stitch into first dc.
Row 2: 3 chain 3tr 3 chain 1 slip stitch into same place as join, * 1 slip stitch 3 chain 3tr 3 chain 1 slip stitch in next stitch, repeat from * twice. [4 petals.]
Work 1 slip stitch in joining stitch, 8 chain, turn and starting with 2nd chain from hook slip stitch back along chain towards flower. Fasten off leaving a long thread to use to attach flower.
Sew on buttons and sew on flowers to both fronts.

Sunday-best bonnet

The perfect accessory to complement the Sunday-best cardigan, this little bonnet has timeless appeal. It is worked in a combination of all the basic stitches with a contrast stitch trim. The bonnet edge is threaded with fine satin ribbon and then finished with wide satin sash bows. Although classic in cream, this bonnet is also oh-so-cute in colour. Make the bonnet as part of a set along with a matching pair of Rosebud Slippers – a gift that will delight all new parents.

Making the Sunday-best bonnet

BONNET SIZE

One size (approximately 13cm from centre of crown to brim) to fit 0–3 months

MATERIALS

2 x 50g balls Rowan Cotton Glace or similar medium-weight cotton yarn (see page 170)
Hook size 3.00mm
Approximately 0.5m fine satin ribbon, 3mm wide
Approximately 1.5m wide satin ribbon, 2.5cm wide

STITCH SIZE

This bonnet has a tension of 16 stitches and 16 rows to 10cm measured over the two row pattern.

TECHNIQUES USED

Double crochet, treble crochet, half treble and double treble crochet and simple shaping and edging (see pattern)

For double crochet:	see page 14
For treble crochet:	see page 16
For half treble crochet:	see page 18
For double treble crochet:	see page 19

METHOD

Foundation chain: Leaving a long loose end, chain 5.

Row 1: 2dc in 2nd chain from hook, [2dc in next chain] repeat to end. Turn. [8 stitches.]

Row 2: Chain 2, [2tr in dc] repeat to last stitch, 1tr in last stitch. Turn. [15 stitches.]

Row 3 and every alternate row: [1 chain, 1dc in next stitch], repeat to end. Turn.

Row 4: Chain 3, [2tr in dc] repeat to end. Turn. [30 stitches.]

Row 6: Chain 3, [2tr in next stitch, 1tr] repeat to end. Turn. [45 stitches.]

Row 8: Chain 3, tr to end. Turn.

Row 10: Chain 3, 2tr, 2tr in next stitch, [3tr, 2tr in next stitch] repeat to last 2 stitches, 2tr. Turn. [56 stitches.]

Row 12: As Row 8.

Row 14: Chain 3, 4tr, [2tr in next stitch, 5tr] repeat to last 4 stitches, 2tr in next stitch, 3tr. Turn. [65 stitches.]

Row 15: [chain 1, 1dc in next stitch] repeat to end. Turn.

Row 16: Chain 3, tr to end. Turn.
Repeat Rows 15 and 16 until work measures 14cm, finishing at the end of a Row 15.

Reverse work as follows:

Next row: [chain 1, 1dc to end. Turn.]

Next row: As Row 16.

Next row: As Row 15.

Repeat last two rows.

Next row: Chain 2, 2 half treble, 2 half treble in next stitch, [3 half treble, 2 half treble in next stitch] 15 times, 2 half treble. Turn. [82 stitches.]

Next row: As Row 15.

Next row: Chain 3, 3 double treble in next stitch, [miss 3dc, 3dc, miss 3dc, 7 double treble in next stitch] repeat to last 10dc, miss 3dc, 3dc, miss 3dc, 4 double treble in last stitch. Turn.

Next row: Chain 1, dc to end.

Fasten off.

TO FINISH

Weave any loose ends into the work.

Lay the work out flat, then steam and press lightly.

Join the seam from the centre of the crown to the end of the shapings.

Turn back the trim. Thread the fine ribbon through the eyelet holes of the trim.

Cut the wide ribbon in half. Make a big bow at one end of each piece and attach one to each side of the bonnet as shown.

Rosebud slippers

There is nothing quite like a pair of tiny slippers to make even the hardest of hearts melt, and even prompt one to take up a hook and learn to crochet. Reminiscent of little dancing shoes, these rosebud slippers are quite irresistible. Made in glazed cotton and worked in single crochet with simple increases and decreases, they are finished with butter-soft suede soles, satin ribbon ties, and dainty crocheted flowers. They are a delight both to make and give.

Making the Rosebud slippers

SLIPPERS SIZE

To fit age (months):	0–3	3–6	6–9
Length:	8cm	9cm	10cm

MATERIALS

1 x 50g ball Rowan Cotton Glace
or similar medium-weight cotton yarn
(see page 170)
Hook size 3.00mm
1.25m fine satin ribbon, 1cm wide
Sewing needle

STITCH SIZE

These slippers have a tension of 6 stitches
and 6 rows to 2.5cm measured over double
crochet using hook size 3.00mm.

TECHNIQUES USED

Double crochet and working in rounds

For double crochet: see page 14

For working in rounds: see page 22

TIPS

The slippers are made in one piece starting
with the sole. Ensure you secure all motifs
very carefully. Take time and care in
checking for any remaining pins once
sewn together.

METHOD

Sole

Foundation chain: Leaving a long loose
end, chain 8.

Row 1: 1dc into 2nd chain from hook,
dc to end. Turn.

Row 2: Chain 1, 2dc into next dc, dc to last
dc, 2dc into last dc. Turn.

Row 3: Chain 1, dc to end. Turn.

Repeat row 3 until work measures 8 (9:
10)cm from start.

Next row: Chain 1, miss 1dc, dc to last
2dc, miss 1dc, 1dc in last dc. Turn.

Upper

Round 1: Chain 1, 7 (7: 7)dc, 14 (16: 18)dc
along side of sole, 7 (7: 7)dc along toe, 14
(16: 18)dc along other side of sole and join
with a slip stitch into 1ch at beg of round.
[42 (46: 50) stitches.]

Round 2: Chain 1, dc to end, join with a
slip stitch into 1st chain.

Repeat Round 2 twice.

Round 5: Chain 1, 20 (22: 24)dc, miss 1dc,

7 (7: 7)dc, miss 1sc, 13 (15: 17)dc, join with slip stitch into 1st chain.

Round 6: Chain 1, 20 (22: 24)dc, miss 1dc, 5 (5: 5)dc, miss 1dc, 13 (15: 17)dc, join with slip stitch into 1st chain.

Round 7: Chain 1, 20 (22: 24)dc, miss 1dc, 3 (3: 3)dc, miss 1dc, 13 (15: 17)dc, join with slip stitch into 1st chain.

Rnd 8: Chain 1, 20 (22: 24)dc, miss 1dc, 1dc, miss 1dc, 13 (15: 17)dc, join with slip stitch into 1st chain.

Round 9: Chain 1, 5dc, 5 chain slip stitch into same stitch to make loop for ribbon, then 11 (13: 15)dc, (miss 1dc, 1dc into next dc) 5 times, dc to end, join with slip stitch into 1st chain. Fasten off.

To make flower (make 2)
Foundation chain: Chain 2.
Row 1: 5dc into 2nd chain from hook, slip stitch into 1st dc.
Row 2: Chain 3, 3tr 3 chain 1 slip stitch into same place as join, * 1 slip stitch in next dc, 3 chain 3tr 3 chain 1 slip stitch in same dc, repeat from * 3 times. [5 petals.] Fasten off.

TO FINISH
Attach a flower to the front of each slipper. Cut the length of ribbon in half and thread through the loop. Tie in a secure bow. Using the sole as a template, trace the outline onto the suede. Cut out 2 pieces and sew onto the bottom of each slipper with a small, neat hand stitches.

Cuddle shawl

Every new baby deserves the best. Crocheted in the softest, most beautiful hand-dyed alpaca yarn, this shawl is pure luxury. The sheer simplicity of the design complements the ultimate softness of the wool and creates an heirloom piece that even the novice will be able to make and be proud of.

Making the Cuddle shawl

For treble crochet: see page 16

For half treble crochet: see page 18

For double treble crochet: see page 19

For triple treble crochet: see page 20

For working in rounds: see page 22

SIZE
Approximately 76cm x 76cm

MATERIALS
8 x 100g hanks Blue Skies Chunky Alpaca or a similar aran-weight wool yarn (see page 170)
Hook sizes 5.50mm and 6.00mm

STITCH SIZE
This shawl has a tension of 11 stitches to 10cm and 4 rows to 7.5cm measured over treble crochet on hook size 6.00mm.

TECHNIQUES USED
Double, treble, half treble, double treble and triple treble crochet and working in rounds

For double crochet: see page 14

TIPS
Working in rounds: When you work in rounds, you never have to turn the fabric. The right side is always facing you.

METHOD
Foundation chain: Leaving a long loose end and using a hook size 6.00mm, chain 6 and join length of chain into ring by working a slip stitch into 1st chain made.

Round 1: Chain 5 (counts as 1tr, 2 chain), [3tr into ring, 2 chain] 3 times, 2tr into ring, slip stitch to 3rd of 5 chain. [4 groups of 3 trebles.]

Round 2: Slip stitch into corner arch, chain 7 (counts as 1tr, 4 chain), * 2tr into same arch, 1tr into each tr across side of square ** , 2tr into next arch, 4 chain, repeat from * twice and from * to ** again, 1tr into same arch as 7 chain, slip stitch to 3rd of 7 chain. [4 groups of 7 trebles.]

Round 3: As Round 2. [4 groups of 11 trebles.]

Round 4: As Round 2. [4 groups of 15 trebles.]

Continue increasing in the same way until 19 rounds have been completed, which will be 4 groups of 75 trebles.

Do not fasten off but continue with border as follows:

Border

Using a hook size 5.00mm, chain 1, 1dc into same place as 1 chain [chain 6, 1dc in 2nd chain from hook, 1 half treble in next chain, 1tr in next chain, 1 double treble in next chain, 1 triple treble in next chain, miss 4 stitches, 1dc in next stitch] repeat all round. Make sure that the triangles sit neatly on the corners by working the dc at the start and end of the triangle within the arch. Fasten off.

TO FINISH

Weave any loose ends into the work. Lay the work out flat, then steam and press lightly.

Vintage

The ultimate in crochet: a collection of personal accessories to create a fashionable vintage look. Dress up in a cascading ruffle scarf, fasten a corsage pin to your lapel and style a delicate freeform crochet camisole with your favourite worn denims. The projects vary from the very simple trio of ribbon bracelets, which can all be made in less than an hour, to the more complex camisole that requires a greater degree of skill and the confidence to experiment.

Ruffle scarf

Add a touch of vintage style to any outfit with this cascading ruffle scarf. Worked in long rounds, it is an extremely quick project to make. Start crocheting it today and you will be wearing the scarf by this evening! I can guarantee that everyone else will want one too, so you are sure to make this scarf pattern time after time – experiment with lots of textures and colours, even in the same scarf, to create something completely individual.

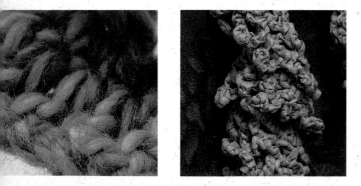

Making the Ruffle scarf

SCARF SIZE
Approximately 145cm long

MATERIALS
3 x 50g balls Rowan R2 Paper Yarn or similar paper yarn (see page 170) OR 3 x 100g balls Rowan Biggy Print or similar chunky wool yarn (see page 170) Hook size 6.00mm for paper yarn OR hook size 8.00mm for wool yarn

STITCH SIZE
Two-pattern repeats to 9cm, when measured along the starting chain. Depth of pattern is 9cm when measured from starting chain to edge of central picot loop.

TECHNIQUES USED
Double and treble crochet

For double crochet: see page 14
For treble crochet: see page 16

TIPS
Tension: Don't worry about tension too much! Because this scarf does not have to be an exact size, you can add stitches until it is the length required.

METHOD
Foundation chain: Working loosely and using hook size 6.00mm with paper yarn and hook size 8.00mm with wool yarn, chain 117.
Row 1: Work 1dc into 3rd chain from hook, then 1dc into each chain to end.

Turn.
Row 2: 5 chain, miss 1st 4dc, slip stitch into next dc, * 5 chain, miss 3 sc, slip stitch into next dc, repeat from * to end. Turn. [29 spaces.]
Row 3: Chain 1 to count as 1st dc, 7dc into 1st 5 chain space, 8dc into each 5 chain space to end.
Repeat rows 2 and 3 along opposite side of foundation chain. Turn.
Round 4: Chain 4 to count as 1st dc and 1 chain, * 1dc, 1 chain into next dc, repeat from * round both sides. Join with slip stitch to 3rd of 4 chain.
For the paper scarf only
Round 5: * 5 chain, miss next space, dc in next space, repeat from * to end of round. Join with slip stitch to base of first loop.

Round 6: Slip stitch across 1st 3 chain of
1st loop, * 6 chain, 1dc in next loop,
repeat from * to end of round. Join with
slip stitch to base of 1st loop.

Round 7 (picot edge): Slip stitch across
1st 3 chain of 1st loop, * 6 chain, 1dc in
3rd chain from hook, 3 chain, 1dc into next
loop, repeat from * to end, slip stitch to
base of 1st loop.

Heart-shaped cushion

The beauty of crochet is its versatility; it can be made in small, easy pieces that may then be assembled in different ways. This pretty heart-shaped cushion is worked in this way. Simple textural stitches are created with very basic shaping and pieced together like a puzzle. They are joined with chains to create large spaces through which the rich satin lining is glimpsed and then further embellished with self-colour motifs. It is finished with a very easy edging to emphasise the heart shape. Adds a little instant glamour to any boudoir!

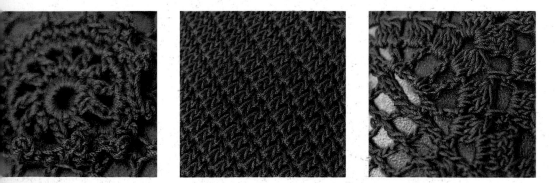

Making the Heart-shaped cushion

CUSHION SIZE
Approximately 48cm x 38cm at widest point

MATERIALS
Approximately 250g Yeomans Cotton Cannele or similar 4-ply mercerised cotton yarn (see page 170)
Hook sizes 2.00mm, 2.50mm and 3.00mm
Graph paper, one square to 1cm
Large sewing needle
Cushion pad

STITCH SIZE
This cushion has a tension of 12 stitches and 5 rows to 5cm measured over trebles.

TECHNIQUES USED
This cushion is made up of various different shapes of crochet using a variety of stitches.

For basic crochet stitches: see pages 14–

TIPS
Before starting work, take time to draw the heart shape onto graph paper. Mark each shape onto your template and crochet to fit these shapes. Pin each piece to the template as you go.

METHOD

Rose bower square for Front
Base ring: With 3.00mm hook, chain 6 and join into a ring with a slip stitch.
Round 1: Chain 5, [1tr into ring, 2 chain] 7 times, slip stitch into 3rd of 5 chain. [8 spaces.]
Round 2: [1dc 1 half treble 3tr 1 half treble 1dc into each space] 8 times, slip stitch into 1st dc. [8 petals.]
Round 3: 1dc into same place as slip stitch,

* 4 chain, 1dc between next 2 petals, repeat from * to end, slip stitch into 1st dc.
Round 4: * 1dc 1 half treble 5tr 1 half treble 1dc into space, repeat from * to end, slip stitch into 1st dc.
Round 5: As Round 3.
Round 6: * 1dc 1 half treble 7tr 1 half treble 1dc into space, repeat from * to end, slip stitch into 1st dc.
Round 7: As Round 3.
Round 8: * 1dc 1 half treble 1tr 7 double treble 1tr 1 half treble 1dc, repeat from * to end, slip stitch into 1st dc.
Round 9: Slip stitch to centre double treble of 1st petal, 1dc in same place as last slip stitch, * 7 chain, leaving the last loop of each double treble on the hook work 3 double treble into centre double treble of next petal, yarn over hook and pull through all loops on hook (cluster made), 4 chain, into same double treble work a 3 double treble cluster 4 chain and a 3 double treble cluster, 7 chain, 1dc into centre double treble of next petal, repeat from * all round, slip stitch into 1st dc.
Round 10: Slip stitch to centre 3 double treble cluster of 1st 3 double treble cluster group, 3 chain, 2tr into same stitch * 1 chain, 3tr into next space, [1 chain, 3tr 1 chain 3tr into next space] twice, 1 chain, 3tr into next space, 1 chain, 3tr 3 chain 3tr into tip of next cluster, repeat from * all round, omitting 3tr 3 chain 3tr at end of last repeat, 3tr into same place as 1st 2tr, 1 chain, 1tr into 3rd of 3 chain.
Rounds 11–13: Chain 3, 2tr into space just formed, * [1 chain, 3tr into next space] 7 times, 1 chain, 3tr 3 chain 3tr into corner space, repeat from * all round, omitting 3tr

3 chain 3tr at end of last repeat, 3tr into same place as 1st 2tr, 1 chain, 1tr into 3rd of 3 chain.
Round 14: As Round 11, omitting 3tr 3 chain 3tr at end of last repeat; 3tr into same place as 1st 2tr, 3 chain, slip stitch to 3rd of 3 chain. Fasten off leaving long end.

Plain motif for Back
Base ring: Using 3.00mm hook, chain 6 and join into a ring with a slip stitch.
Round 1: Chain 5 (count as 1tr and 2 chain), [3tr into ring, 2 chain] 3 times, 2tr into ring, slip stitch to 3rd of 5 chain. [4 groups of 3tr.]
Round 2: Slip stitch into corner arch, 7 chain (count as 1tr and 4 chain), * 2tr into same arch, 1tr into each tr across side of square **, 2tr into next arch, 4 chain, repeat from * twice and from * to ** again, 1tr into same arch as 7 chain, slip stitch to 3rd of 7 chain. [4 groups of 7tr.]
Round 3: As Round 2. [4 groups of 11tr.]
Round 4: As Round 2. [4 groups of 15tr.]
Continue increasing in the same way until 11 rounds have been completed which will be 4 groups of 43tr.

Crossed treble sections for Front and Back (make 2)
Two crossed trebles: Miss next stitch, 1tr into next stitch, 1tr into missed stitch working over previous treble.
Foundation row: Using 3.00mm hook, chain 36.
Row 1: Miss 3 chain (count as 1tr), * 2 crossed treble over next 2 chain, repeat from * ending 1tr into last chain. Turn.
Row 2: Chain 1 (count as 1dc), miss 1

stitch, 1dc into next and each stitch to end, working last stitch into top of turning chain.

Row 3: Chain 3 (count as 1tr), miss 1 stitch, * work 2 crossed treble over next 2 stitches, repeat from * ending 1tr into turning chain. Turn.

Repeat Rows 2 and 3 until work measures 11cm ending with a Row 2.

Shape top by working 3tr together at end of every crossed treble row [i.e. decreasing 2 stitches at end of row], and decrease 1 stitch at beginning of every dc row by working 2dc together. Continue decreasing like this until 1 stitch left.

Fasten off leaving long end.

Filet sections for Front and Back (make 2)

Foundation chain: Using 2.50mm hook, chain 44.

Row 1: 1tr in 8th chain from hook, * 2 chain, miss 2 stitches of base chain, 1tr, repeat from * to end. [13 squares in total.]

Row 2: Chain 5, * 1tr into tr, 2 chain, repeat from * to end of row working 1tr into 3rd chain stitch of previous row. Repeat row 2 until work measures 12.5cm. Shape top by decreasing 1 block at each end of every row until 1 block remains. Fasten off leaving long end.

Heart tops for Front and Back (make 4)

Base ring: Using 2.50mm hook, chain 12 and join into a ring with a slip stitch to 1st chain.

Row 1: Chain 5 [1 double treble into ring, 1 chain] 5 times, 1 double treble into ring. Turn.

Row 2: Chain 5, * leaving last loop of each stitch on hook work 4tr into next 1 chain space, yarn round hook and draw through 5 loops on hook (cluster made), 2 chain, repeat from * into each space all round, ending with 1 cluster into space formed by turning chain, 2 chain, 1tr into 3rd turning chain. Turn.

Row 3: Chain 5, 4tr into 1st 2 chain space, * [3 chain, 1dc into next 2 chain space] twice, 3 chain **, 4tr 2 chain 4tr into next 2 chain space, repeat from * to ** once more, 4tr into space formed by turning chain, 2 chain, 1tr into 3rd turning chain. Turn.

Row 4: Chain 5, 4tr into 1st 2 chain space, 1 chain, miss 1st 3 chain space, * [4tr into next 3 chain space, 1 chain] twice **, [4tr, 2 chain, 4tr] into next 2 chain space, 1 chain, repeat from * to ** once more, 4tr into space formed by turning chain, 2 chain, 1tr into 3rd turning chain. Turn.

Row 5: Chain 4, 4tr into 1st 2 chain space, * [4tr into next 1 chain space] 3 times **,

4tr 2 chain 4tr into next 2 chain space, repeat from * to ** once more, 4tr into space formed by turning chain, 1 chain, 1tr into 3rd turning chain. Turn.
Continue until triangle is required size. Fasten off leaving long end.

TO MAKE UP CUSHION

Pin pieces to heart-shaped template and sew together while still pinned to the paper. This helps to keep the shape.
Using 2.50mm hook, work round the edge as follows starting at the bottom point of the heart: 36dc along edge of square motif, 28 chain across gap, 31dc along crossed treble section, 124dc across top of heart, 31dc along filet section, 28 chain across gap and 36dc along second edge of square motif. Work another row dc, working 1dc into every dc and 1dc into each chain across gaps.
With wrong sides together, oversew the two pieces half way around, insert cushion pad and finish sewing.
Fill in the gaps with the following motifs:

Magic circles (make 2)
Base ring: Using 2.50mm hook, chain 16 and join into a ring with a slip stitch.
Round 1: Chain 2 (counts as 1 half treble), 35 half treble into ring, join with slip stitch to 2nd of 1 chain at beginning of round.
Round 2: Chain 1, 1dc into same stitch as last slip stitch, * 5 chain, miss 2 half treble, 1dc into next half treble, repeat from * 10 times, 5 chain, slip stitch into 1st dc. Fasten off leaving long end.

Lace triangle (make 2)
Base ring: Wind yarn round little finger to form a ring.
Round 1: Using 2.50mm hook, chain 1,

12dc into ring, slip stitch to 1st dc.
Round 2: Chain 10 (count as 1tr 7 chain), miss 1st 2dc, * 1tr into next dc, 3 chain, miss 1dc, 1tr, 7 chain, miss 1dc, repeat from * once, 1tr, 3 chain, miss last sc, slip stitch to 3rd of 10 chain.
Round 3: 3 chain [count as 1tr], 3tr 7 chain 4tr into next chain arch, * 3tr into next chain arch, 4tr 7 chain 4tr into next chain arch, repeat from * once, 3tr into last chain arch, slip stitch to top of 3 chain.
Fasten off leaving long end.

Lace edging
Base ring: Using 2.00mm hook, chain 6.
Row 1: 1tr into 4th chain from hook and into next of next 2 chain leaving the last loop of each on hook, yarn over hook and draw through all loops on hook (cluster made), 5 chain, 1tr into single loop of 5th chain from hook, [2 chain, 1tr into same place] 4 times, 1 triple treble into same place as last tr of cluster, 7 chain. Turn.
Row 2: Miss 1st tr, 1dc into next tr, 3 chain. Turn.
Row 3: 1tr into each of 1st 3 of 7 turning chain leaving the last loop of each on hook and complete a cluster as before, 5 chain, 1tr into single loop of 5th chain from hook, [2 chain, 1tr in same place] 4 times, 1 triple treble into same place as last tr of cluster, 7 chain. Turn.
Repeat Rows 2 and 3 until lace fits around the outside edge of the pillow.

TO FINISH
Pin the lace edging all around the outside edge of the pillow and hand sew into position, accentuating its heart shape. Crochet as many of the following motifs as preferred and attach to front of cushion.

Wheel motif
Base ring: With 2.5mm hook, chain 6 and join into a ring with a slip stitch.
Round 1: Chain 1, 12dc into ring, slip stitch to 1st dc.
Round 2: Chain 4, * 1tr, 1 chain, repeat from * to end, slip stitch to 3rd of 4 chain.
Round 3: Chain 1, * 3dc in next chain space, repeat from * to end, slip stitch to 1st dc.
Round 4: * Chain 4, slip stitch to 1st chain to make picot, 3dc, repeat from * to end, slip stitch to base of 1st picot. Fasten off.

Trefoil motif
Round 1: With 2.50mm hook, chain 16, slip stitch into 1st chain (1st loop formed), [15 chain, slip stitch into same chain as last slip stitch] twice.
Round 2: Chain 1, * 28dc into next loop, slip stitch into same chain as slip stitch of Round 1, repeat from * twice.
Round 3: Slip stitch into each of 1st 3dc, 1 chain, 1dc into same stitch as last slip stitch, 23dc, * miss 4dc, 24dc, repeat from * once. Fasten off leaving long thread.

Flower motif
Foundation row: Using 3.50mm hook, chain 2.
Row 1: 4dc into 2nd chain from hook, slip stitch into 1st dc.
Row 2: 3 chain, 3tr 3 chain 1 slip stitch into same place as join, * 1 slip stitch, 3 chain 3tr 3 chain 1 slip stitch in next dc, repeat from * 3 times. [4 petals made.]
Work 1 slip stitch in joining stitch, 8 chain, turn, starting with 2nd chain from hook slip stitch back along chain towards flower. Fasten off leaving long thread.

Corsage pin

Corsages are currently an extremely popular accessory, taking their inspiration from vintage apparel.

It can be made in a variety of yarns, colours and textures, with various decorative embellishments.

It is the perfect small project to personalise an outfit and makes an ideal gift for a cherished friend.

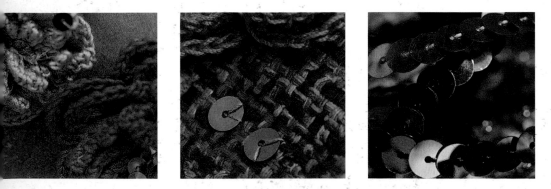

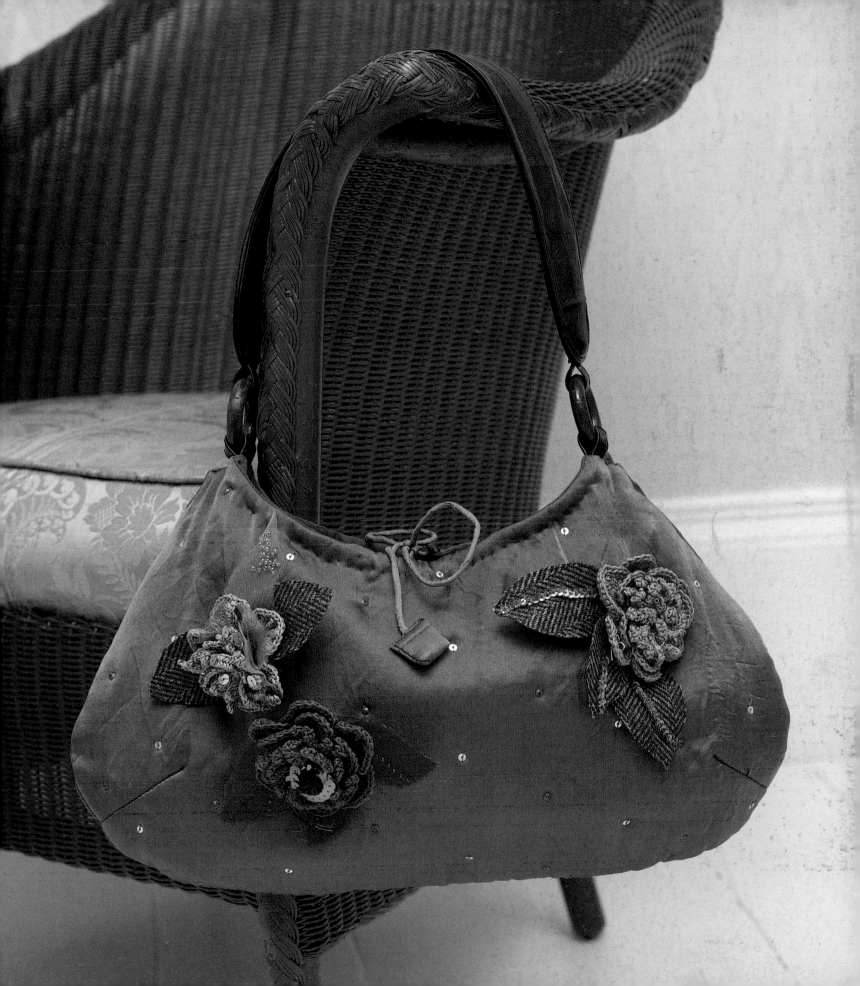

Making the Corsage pin

CORSAGE SIZE

Approximately 7cm in diameter without leaves. Make the flowers larger or smaller by using a larger or smaller crochet hook.

MATERIALS

Small amount of Yeomans Cotton Cannele or similar 4-ply mercerised cotton yarn (see page 170)
Hook size 1.50mm
Scraps of fabric, such as tweed, for leaves
Scraps of felt, for backing
Sequins
Sewing needle and thread
Safety pin

TECHNIQUES USED

Double, treble, half treble and double treble crochet and working in rounds

| For double crochet: see page 14 |
| For treble crochet: see page 16 |
| For half treble crochet: see page 18 |
| For double treble crochet: see page 19 |
| For working in rounds: see page 22 |

METHOD

Large flower

Base ring: Chain 6 and join into a ring with a slip stitch into 1st chain.

Round 1: Chain 5, [1tr, 2 chain] 5 times into ring, slip stitch to 3rd of 5 chain at beginning of round.

Round 2: [Chain 7, 1dc in 2nd chain between trebles] 6 times, slip stitch to base of 1st loop. [6 spaces made.]

Round 3: Into each space work 1dc 1 half treble 2tr 4 double treble 5 triple treble 4 double treble 2tr 1 half treble 1dc. Fasten off.

Medium flower

Base ring: Chain 6 and join into a ring with a slip stitch into 1st chain.

Round 1: Work as Round 1 given for Large flower.

Round 2: Work as Round 2 given for Large flower.

Round 3: Into each space work 1dc 1 half treble 2tr 9 double treble 2tr 1 half treble 1dc.
Fasten off.

Small flower

Base ring: Chain 6 and join into a ring by working a slip stitch into 1st chain made.

Round 1: Work as Round 1 given for Large flower.

Round 2: Work as Round 2 given for Large flower.

Round 3: Into each space work 1dc 1 half treble 8tr 1 half treble 1dc. Fasten off.

Stamens

Base ring: Chain 4 and join into a ring with a slip stitch into 1st chain.

Round 1: 13dc into ring, slip stitch to 1st dc at beginning of round.

Round 2: Working into front strand only of each dc of Round 1, work 1sc, * chain 5, 1sc in 2nd chain from hook, 2 half treble, 1dc, 1dc in next dc of Round 1 (1 petal made), repeat from * 12 times. [13 petals.]

Round 3: Work into back strand only of each dc of Round 1, work 1 slip stitch, * chain 6, 5dc, 1 slip stitch in next dc of Round 1, repeat from * 12 times. [13 petals]. Fasten off.

TO FINISH

Layer two different sized flowers – large and medium, or medium and small – one on top of the other. Slip stitch together. Place the stamens in centre and secure with small, neat hand stitches.

Cut out some basic leaf shapes from the scraps of fabric. Arrange the leaves underneath the flower and sew into position.

Cut out a small circle of felt and stick or sew it to the back of the corsage and attach a safety pin.

Freeform camisole

This pretty camisole is worked in freeform crochet. It is semi-fitted with an asymmetrical hem, contrast shell-stitch bodice and fashionable double straps. Freeform crochet is worked in a very different way, as you create the fabric much more freely to your own pattern. This lingerie-inspired top is based on a favourite underpiece, which was simply traced onto a piece of paper to create a template and an asymmetrical hem added for design measure. Alternatively, you could use bought paper pattern and crochet to fit that. The basic instructions are given here in one size; it is a guideline for you to take as the inspiration to create a uniquely personal piece.

Making the Freeform camisole

CAMISOLE SIZE
One size (to fit up to bust 92cm), but size can be easily adjusted as required

MATERIALS
Approximately 250g Yeomans Cotton Cannele or similar 4-ply mercerised cotton yarn (see page 170)
Hook size 3.00mm
Approximately 1m satin ribbon, 5mm wide

STITCH SIZE
This camisole has a tension of 20 chains to 8cm, but working to an exact tension is not essential (see Tips).

TECHNIQUES USED
Double, treble and half treble crochet and working in rounds.

For double crochet: see page 16

For treble crochet: see page 18

For half treble crochet: see page 19

For working in rounds: see page 22

For freeform crochet: see page 24

TIPS
Tension: Don't worry about tension too much! If your motifs ends up a bit bigger or smaller than the size given here, just add more motifs to achieve the required size.

METHOD
Sketch out the basic camisole shape for your design or trace around a favourite garment to actual size onto squared paper to make a template.

Bodice stitch
Work in multiples of 5 with 6 turning chain.
Foundation row: 4tr 2 chain 1tr in 7th chain from hook, * miss 4 chain, 4tr 2 chain 1tr in next chain, repeat from * to end of row ending with 2 missed chains, 1tr in last chain, 3 chain to turn.
Row 1: * 4tr 2 chain 1tr in 2 chain space, repeat from * to end of row ending with 1tr in turning chain, 3 chain to turn.
Repeat Row 1.
Shape the bodice as required, referring to your pattern template.
On the lower edge of the front bodice make a chain to decrease the edge to measure 40cm when finished.
Pin each piece of the bodice onto the pattern template in turn.

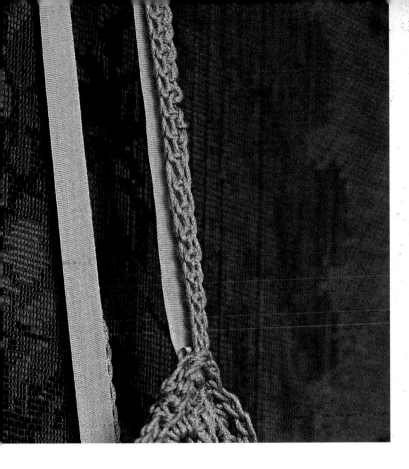

Front freeform crochet

Crochet as many of the following motifs as required:

Rosette A

Base ring: Chain 7, join with slip stitch.
Round 1: Chain 1, 12dc into ring, join with slip stitch into 1st dc, 3 chain.
Round 2: 1tr into next stitch, * 3 chain, 2tr, repeat from * 4 times, 3 chain, join with slip stitch to top of 3 chain.

Rosette B

Base ring: Chain 6, join with slip stitch.
Round 1: Chain 1, 16dc into ring, slip stitch to 1st dc.
Round 2: Chain 6, miss 2 stitches, * 1tr, 3 chain, miss 1 stitch, repeat from * 6 times, slip stitch to 3rd chain of 6 chain.
Round 3: Chain 1, * 1dc 1 half treble 5tr 1 half treble 1dc in 3 chain space, repeat from * 7 times, slip stitch to 1st dc.

Rosette C

Base ring: Chain 10, join with slip stitch.
Round 1: 24dc into ring, slip stitch into 1st dc.
Round 2: [Chain 6, miss 2dc, 1dc, repeat from * 7 times, slip stitch into 1st chain.
Round 3: * 8dc into next 6 chain space, repeat from * 7 times, slip stitch into 1st dc.

Rosette D

Base ring: Chain 10, join with slip stitch.
Round 1: 24 half treble into ring, slip stitch into 1st half treble.

Rosette E

Base ring: Chain 6, join with slip stitch.
Row 1: Chain 1, 18dc into ring, 6 chain. Turn.
Row 2: Miss 2 stitches, * 1tr, 3 chain, miss 1 stitch, repeat from * 3 times. Turn.
Row 3: Chain 1, * 1dc 1 half treble 5tr 1 half treble 1dc in 3 chain space, repeat from * 3 times.

TO FINISH

Pin each motif onto the pattern template as preferred to create a pleasing arrangement. Draw chain lines onto the paper template between all the motifs to link them together.

Crochet linking chains between motifs
following the drawn lines, leaving the
motifs pinned to the pattern template.
Insert groups of trebles at the points where
two or more chains cross.

Straps

Make two lengths of chain to attach to the
peaks of the bodice, from front to back.
Repeat for the back body piece.
Sew body and bodice along the side seams.
Attach crochet straps together with silk
ribbon straps.
Thread a length of thin silk ribbon along
the base of the bodice if desired. Tie into a
small, neat bow.

Beaded handbag

Not exclusively for evenings out, this little handbag is suitable to be used at any time of day. It is small enough to look dressy but practical enough to keep your keys, mobile and lipstick to hand. Tiny glass beads are threaded onto mercerised cotton and crocheted in simple double crochet. The finished effect is vintage, especially when using tones of one colour such as old rose, gunmetal or biscuit. Contrast this with bamboo or tortoiseshell handles and line with a pretty paisley print or a fabric taken from an old shirt or dress from your favourite thrift store. Finish off the bag with a rosette, using either the pattern for the corsage pin or the flowers from the contemporary pillows.

Making the Beaded handbag

HANDBAG SIZE
23cm x 28cm measured from centre of side gusset to centre of opposite side gusset and from gusset to end of turnover for handles.

MATERIALS
200g Yeomans Cotton Cannele or similar 4-ply mercerised cotton yarn (see page 170)
Approximately 1200 beads
Hook size 2.00mm and 3.00mm
Fabric, such as chiffon, for lining
Bamboo D handles (or similar)
Large sewing needle and thread

STITCH SIZE
This handbag has a tension of 24 stitches and 32 rows to 10cm measured over doubles using a 3.00mm hook.

TECHNIQUES USED
Double crochet and crocheting in beads (see pattern)

For double crochet: see page 14

TIPS
Adding a bead in single crochet: Insert the hook through the stitch of the previous row in the usual way, yarn round hook and draw a loop through. Then slide the bead close to the work, yarn round hook and draw through both loops at the same time pushing the bead firmly on top of the stitch in the previous row.

METHOD
Side (make 2)
Before starting the work, thread approximately half the beads onto the yarn.
Foundation chain: Using 3.00mm hook, chain 69.
Row 1: 1dc in 2nd chain from hook, 1dc in each chain to end, 1 chain. Turn.
Row 2: 1dc in each dc to end, 1 chain. Turn.
Row 3: As Row 2.
Next row (wrong side): 2dc, * add a bead with next and every alternate dc, 1dc, repeat from * to last 3 stitches, 3dc, 1 chain. Turn.
Next row: As Row 2.
Repeat last 2 rows until work measures 22.5cm.
Change to 2.00mm hook and work 6 rows dc without adding any beads.
Fasten off.

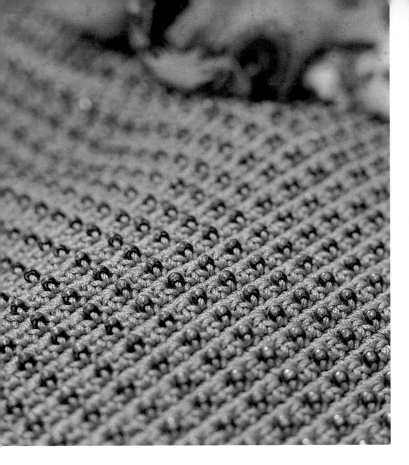

Base

Foundation row: Using 3.00mm hook, chain 57.

Row 1: 1dc in 2nd chain from hook, dc to end, 1 chain. Turn.

Work 15 rows in dc. Fasten off.

Corsage

Thread 26 beads onto yarn.

Base ring: Using 2.00mm hook, chain 4 and join into a ring with a slip stitch.

Round 1: 13dc into ring, slip stitch to 1st dc at beginning of round.

Round 2: Using the front strand only of each dc work petal as follows: 1dc, * 5 chain, attach bead, 1dc in 2nd chain from hook, 2 half treble, 1dc in next chain, 1dc in next dc on Round 1 (1 petal made), repeat from * 12 times. [13 petals.]

Round 3: Using the back strand only of each dc of Round 1 work petal as follows: 1 slip stitch, * 6 chain, attach bead, 5dc, 1 slip stitch in next dc of Round 1, repeat from * 12 times. [13 petals.]
Fasten off.

TO FINISH

Lay the work out flat, then steam and press lightly.

Take fabric for lining and cut out to size of crochet work adding 2cm seam allowance all the way round.

Cut a strip of fabric approximately 50cm by 10cm for the corsage.

With wrong sides together, fold crochet work in half and oversew or graft together the side seams.

With right sides together, fold lining fabric in half and sew both side seams, insert lining into bag and catch at the bottom corners.

In turn, lay the handles on each side and gather fabric through from right side to inside enclosing the top of the lining and the bar of a handle, and secure with small, neat hand stitches to hem.

Take the strip of fabric for the corsage and fold in half lengthways. Gather up this strip into a fan – use a running stitch along the bottom edge to gather. Allow any frayed edges to show along the outer edge.

Sew the fabric corsage into position on the bag. Place the crocheted corsage on top and attach to the bag.

Crocheted bracelets

An irresistible trio of bracelets to crochet for you and all your girl friends. As they can be made from odd remnants of yarn, and each bracelet can be made in less than hour, they make the perfect first crochet project. Experiment with different coloured ribbons, yarns, beads and charms to make a selection of bracelets that will accessorise all your favourite outfits.

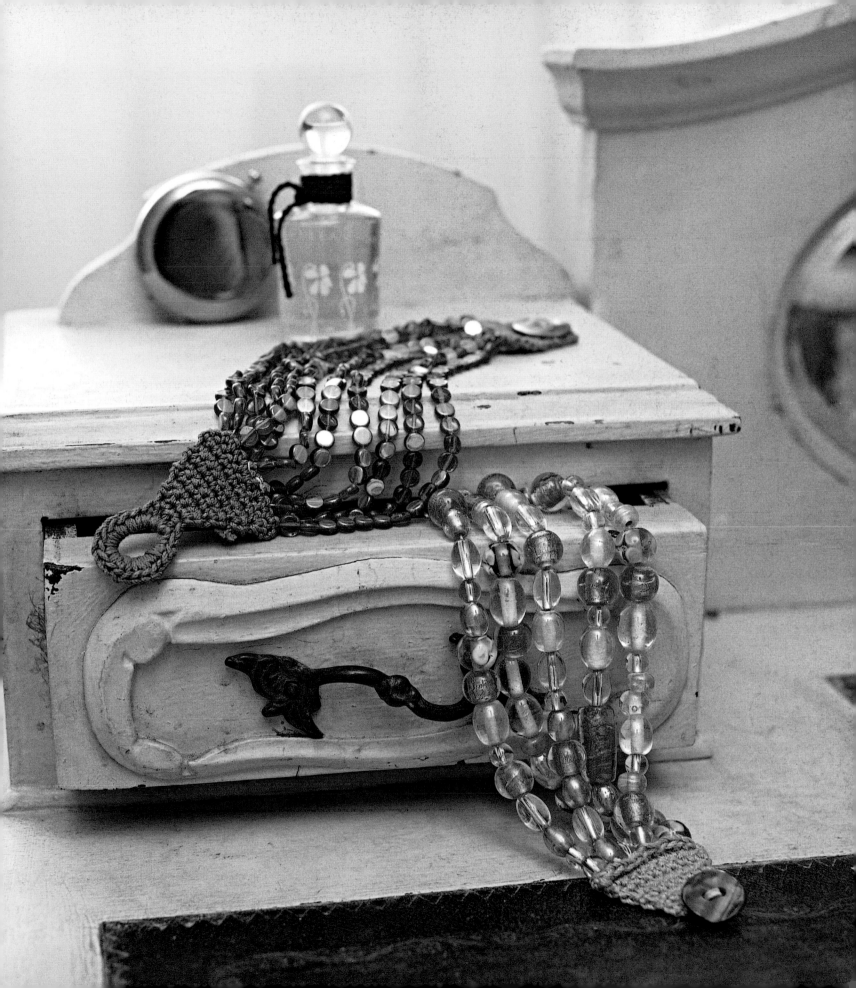

Making the Crocheted bracelets

BRACELET SIZE
All approximately 20cm finished length.

STITCH SIZE
Don't worry about tension too much!
Because these bracelets do not have to be
an exact size, you can add stitches until
they are the length required.

TECHNIQUES USED
Double crochet, cluster stitch, bobble stitch
and crocheting in charms (see pattern)

For double crochet: see page 14

RIBBON CHARM BRACELET

MATERIALS
Approximately 3m satin ribbon, 5mm wide
Approximately 0.5m satin ribbon, 5mm
wide, in a contrast colour
Hook size 3.50mm
10 charms, buttons or beads
Lurex polyester sewing thread

METHOD
Before starting to work, thread the charms
onto the lurex sewing thread in the order
that you want them attached. Work with
the ribbon and lurex thread together,
adding the charms as you crochet.
Leaving a long end for the bracelet tie,
adding a charm at any point, make a cluster
as follows:
* Chain 4, yarn round hook, put hook
through 3rd chain from hook, yarn round
hook, pull through work, yarn round hook,
pull through 2 loops on hook, yarn round
hook, put hook through same space as
before, yarn round hook, pull through work,
yarn round hook and pull through 2 loops
on hook, yarn round hook and pull through
all 3 loops on hook (1 cluster made), repeat
from * 5 times to make 6 clusters.
Fasten off leaving a long end.
Cut the contrast ribbon in half.
Double one piece and link this into same
place as long length of ribbon at start
of bracelet.
Repeat with second piece of contrast ribbon
linking it to the other end of bracelet.

BEADED BRACELET

MATERIALS
Small amount of Yeomans Cotton Canelle or similar 4-ply mercerised cotton yarn (see page 170)
Hook size 1.50mm
Beads or charms
Strong sewing thread and sewing needle
Button

METHOD
Button end
Foundation row: Chain 4.
Row 1: 1dc in 2nd chain from hook, 1dc in each chain to end. (3 stitches). [Turn each row with 1 chain.]
Increase 1 stitch at each end of next and every alternate row until there are 11 dc. Work 1 row dc. Fasten off.

Buttonhole end
Base ring: Chain 10 and join into a ring with a slip stitch.
Work 20dc into ring and join with slip stitch.
Next row: Work 1dc into next 3 stitches, 1 chain, turn. [Turn each row with 1 chain.] Increase 1 stitch at each end of next and every alternate row until there are 11 dc. Work 1 row dc. Fasten off.

TO FINISH
Weave in any long ends.
Secure one end of the thread to the wide end of a triangle and thread the beads or charms to length required to fit around wrist – approximately 15cm – and secure tightly to correspond to the wide end of the other triangle. Thread approximately 5 rows in this manner.
Attach button.

MOTIF BRACELET

MATERIALS
Small amount Yeomans Cotton Cannele or similar 4-ply mercerised cotton yarn (see page 170)
Hook size 2.50mm
6 buttons, assorted sizes
2 x 60cm lengths satin ribbon, 3mm wide, in contrasting colours

METHOD
Bobble stitch: Work 5tr into next dc until 1 loop of each remains on hook, yarn over hook through all 6 loops on hook.
Base ring: Chain 6 and join into a ring with a slip stitch into 1st chain.
Round 1: Chain 1, work 12dc into ring, slip stitch into 1st dc.
Round 2: Chain 3, 4tr into same stitch as last slip stitch until 1 loop of each treble remains on hook, yarn over hook and pull through all 5 loops on hook [1 bobble made at beginning of round], * 5 chain, miss 1dc, 1 bobble into next dc, repeat from * 4 times, 5 chain, slip stitch into top of 1st bobble. [6 bobbles in total.]
Fasten off leaving a long thread.
Make 4 or 5 motifs as required to fit wrist.

TO FINISH
Weave in any yarn ends.
Attach the motifs together to make a band. Thread the two lengths of ribbon through each motif in succession and, at each end, finish with three buttons of various sizes, tying a knot between each button.
Simply knot the ribbon to secure.

Helpful hints for beginners

The section How to Crochet on pages 6–25 shows you how to work the basic stitches in crochet. The following information may be helpful to you when creating crochet projects, either from this book or any other patterns you find.

You can choose to use the recommended yarns, or you can substitute others (see page 170 for information on yarn weights and types so you can choose suitable alternatives). Whether you choose to use the recommended yarns, or ones of your own choice, you must check that you are working to the appropriate tension, or the item you are making may turn out a very different size! Having said that, if you are making a throw, for example, and do not mind too much if it is a little bigger or smaller than the one shown in the pattern, then do not worry too much about stitch size. This is true of cushions, too, unless you wish to create a cover to fit a specific-size cushion pad, when, of course, the tension and the finished size will be important.

Certain yarns are easier to crochet with than others; those that are pliable and soft on the hands are the best for beginners, so select projects with soft cotton yarns to start with. Crocheting with string (or twine) is not difficult, but as it is less pliable than cotton it takes a little more dexterity initially, as indeed does leather, which benefits from being warmed before use.

Pattern information

The instructions for crochet projects are usually given in writing. The basic abbreviations used in pattern writing are shown here, although these can vary, so always check the abbreviations guide in any crochet book first. One area of potential confusion is that U.K. terminology is different from U.S. terminology. In the U.S., double crochet is called single crochet, for example, while treble crochet is known as double crochet, and so on.

In some instances in crochet it is easier to present the pattern information in charted form. This is particularly true of filet crochet where the pattern forms a grid, and can be most easily understood from a chart drawn on graph paper. Each 'block' or 'space' is represented by one square of the graph. Most patterns have elements that repeat. There is an asterisk at the beginning of the repeat element of the pattern, or it is placed inside two asterisks or brackets. The number of times this sequence is repeated is indicated outside the asterisks or brackets, along with any additional stitches required to complete a row.

Practice makes perfect

You will find that the speed and ease with which you crochet is simply a matter of practice. It is a good idea to test your skills on very simple stitches, possibly making a few tension swatches first. (You can always stitch them together later to make a patchwork cushion!)

Abbreviations

To make the instructions for the crochet patterns easier to follow for beginners, very few abbreviations have been used in the book. However, the following lists cover the main abbreviations you may come across in other crochet patterns as well:

abbreviations for crochet stitches

ch	chain
dc	double crochet
dtr	double treble
hdc	half double
sc	single crochet
sl st	slip stitch
tr	treble
trtr	triple treble

other abbreviations

alt	alternate
approx	approximately
beg	begin(ning)
cm	centimeter(s)
cont	continu(e)(ing)
dec	decreas(e)(ing)
foll	follow(s)(ing)
g	gram(s)
in	inch(es)
inc	increas(e)(ing)
m	meter(s)
mm	millimeter(s)
oz	ounce(s)
pat(s)	pattern(s)
rem	remain(s)(ing)
rep	repeat(s)(ing)
RS	right side
st(s)	stitch(es)
tog	together

Caring for crochet

WS   wrong side
yd   yard(s)
yo   yarn over (hook)
*   Repeat instructions after an asterisk or between asterisks as many times as instructed.
[ ]   Repeat instructions inside brackets as many times as instructed.

crochet hooks

Here is a conversion chart for the various systems of hook sizes – just in case you have old hooks you'd like to use but aren't sure what they are equivalent to.

hook conversion chart

Metric	U.S.	old U.K.
.60mm	14 steel	
.75mm	12 steel	
1.00mm	11 steel	
1.50mm	8 steel	
1.75mm	6 steel	
2.00mm	B/1	14
2.50mm	C/2	12
3.00mm	D/3	10
3.50mm	E/4	9
4.00mm	F/5	8
4.50mm	G/6	7
5.00mm	H/8	6
5.50mm	I/9	5
6.00mm	J/10	4
6.50mm		3
7.00mm	K/101/2	2
8.00mm	L/11	
9.00mm	N/13	
10.00mm	P/15	

If you have taken the time and trouble to create your own crochet textiles, you will want to make sure that they remain in good condition. The great variety of yarns on the market has necessitated some kind of international labeling standards for their care, which is usually indicated on the ball band. While some yarns can be successfully dry cleaned (check the symbols on the ball bands), many more are better washed carefully by hand. A few can be machine washed at appropriate temperatures. Again, all this information should be on the ball band.

General hand washing guidelines

• If the article requires hand washing, then make sure that you use gentle soap flakes which must be dissolved before emersing it. Do not use very hot water to wash any wool yarn. Hand-hot temperatures are best.

• Always rinse the article at least twice in tepid water.

• Don't wring it roughly by hand; it is best to give it a short spin in the machine or, with delicate yarns, to wrap it in a towel and squeeze out the moisture gently.

• Pull the article gently into shape and hang it over a towel to dry, preferable on a flat surface.

General machine washing guidelines

The temperature guidelines found on machines are as follows:
140°F/60°C hot: Hotter than the hand can bear; the temperature of most domestic hot water
120°F/50°C hand hot: As hot as the hand can stand
104°F/40°C warm: Just warm to the touch
86°F/30°C cool: Cool to the touch

Care of special yarns

• Mercerised cotton, soft cotton and fine cotton are best washed by hand. Rinse well. Squeeze gently in a towel to remove surplus moisture and hang flat to dry.

• Heavy-weight cottons can be washed in a machine on a cool wash; check the yarn label. Short spin only. Dry flat.

• Lurex, mohair and chenille are best dry cleaned in certain solvents. Check with your dry cleaner. Air well after cleaning.

• String, leather, sisal, hemp and raffia cannot normally be dry cleaned and are best sponged down with a damp cloth and left to dry naturally.

Substituting yarns

Although I have recommended a specific Rowan yarn for many of the projects in the book, you can substitute others. A description of each of the yarns used is given below.

If you decide to use an alternative yarn, any other make of yarn that is of the same weight and type should serve as well, but to avoid disappointing results, it is very important that you test the yarn first. Purchase a substitute yarn that is as close as possible to the original in thickness, weight and texture so that it will be compatible with the crochet instructions. Buy only one ball to start with, so you can try out the effect. Calculate the number of balls you will need by meterage rather than by weight. The recommended knitting-needle size and knitting tension on the ball bands are extra guides to the yarn thickness.

Rowan Yarns

Rowan Kidsilk Haze
A light-weight blend yarn
Recommended knitting-needle size:
3.25–5mm
Tension: 18–25 stitches x 23–24 rows per 10cm over knitted stocking stitch
Ball size: 210m per 25g ball
Yarn specification: 70% super kid mohair, 30% silk

Rowan Cotton Glace
A medium-weight (between double-knitting and 4-ply) mercerised cotton yarn
Recommended knitting-needle size:
3–3.25mm
Tension: 23 stitches x 32 rows per 10cm over knitted stocking stitch
Ball size: 115m per 50g ball
Yarn specification: 100% cotton

Rowan Wool Cotton
A double-knitting weight blend yarn
Recommended knitting-needle size:
3.75–4mm
Tension: 22–24 stitches x 30–32 rows per 10cm over knitted stocking stitch
Ball size: 113m per 50g ball
Yarn specification: 50% merino wool, 50% cotton

Rowan Big Wool
A bulky-weight wool yarn
Recommended knitting-needle size:
15mm
Tension: 7.5 stitches x 10 rows per 10cm over knitted stocking stitch
Ball size: 80m per 100g ball
Yarn specification: 100% merino wool

Rowan Summer Tweed
An Aran-weight blend yarn
Recommended knitting-needle size:
5mm
Tension: 16 stitches x 23 rows per 10cm over knitted stocking stitch
Ball size: 108m per 50g ball
Yarn specification: 70% silk, 30% cotton

Rowan Yorkshire Tweed Aran
An Aran-weight wool yarn
Recommended knitting-needle size:
5–5.5mm
Tension: 16 stitches x 23 rows per 10cm over knitted stocking stitch
Ball size: 160m per 100g ball
Yarn specification: 100% wool

Rowan Chunky Cotton Chenille
A bulky-weight cotton chenille yarn
Recommended knitting-needle size:
4–5mm
Tension: 14–16 stitches x 23–24 rows per 10cm over knitted stocking stitch
Ball size: 140m per 100g ball
Yarn specification: 100% cotton

Rowan Polar
An bulky-weight blend yarn
Recommended knitting-needle size:
8mm
Tension: 12 stitches x 16 rows per 10cm over knitted stocking stitch
Ball size: 100m per 100g ball
Yarn specification: 60% wool, 30% alpaca, 10% acrylic

Rowan RYC Cashsoft Double Knitting
An double-knitting weight blend yarn
Recommended knitting-needle size:
4mm
Tension: 22 stitches x 30 rows per 10cm over knitted stocking stitch
Ball size: 130m per 50g ball
Yarn specification: 57% fine merino wool, 33% microfibre, 10% cashmere

Rowan Biggy Print
An Aran-weight wool yarn
Recommended knitting-needle size:
20mm
Tension: 5.5 stitches x 7 rows per 10cm
over knitted stocking stitch
Ball size: 30m per 100g ball
Yarn specification: 100% wool

Rowan R2 Paper Yarn
An Aran-weight nylon yarn
Recommended knitting-needle size:
8mm
Tension: 14 stitches x 17 rows per 10cm
over knitted stocking stitch
Ball size: 135m per 50g ball
Yarn specification: 100% nylon

Other Yarns

**Jaeger Extra Fine Merino
Double Knitting**
An double-knitting weight wool yarn
Recommended knitting-needle size:
3.25–4mm
Tension: 22 stitches x 30–32 rows per 10cm
over knitted stocking stitch
Ball size: 125m per 50g ball
Yarn specification: 100% fine merino wool

Blue Skies Chunky Alpaca
A bulky-weight wool yarn
Recommended knitting-needle size:
7mm
Tension: 16 stitches per 10cm over knitted
stocking stitch
Ball size: 95m per 100g ball
Yarn specification: 50% merino, 50% alpaca

Fine cotton thread specially designed
for crochet lace is widely available in craft
stores. The cotton thread used for the
Lacy Pillowslip Edgings (pages 62–5),
Organic Table Runner (pages 102–105),
Heart-shaped Pillow (pages 142–7),
Corsage Pin (pages 148–51), Freeform
Camisole Top (pages 152–7), Beaded
Handbag (pages 158–61) and Crocheted
Bracelets (pages 162–5) was obtained from:
Yeoman Yarns Ltd.
36 Churchill Way
Fleckney
Leicestershire LE8 8UD
Tel: +44 (0)116 240 4464
www.yeoman-yarns.co.uk

Leather thonging is available in craft
stores or from leather merchants/saddlery
shops. The 1.5mm-thick round leather
thonging used for the Leather Tote Bag
(pages 44–7) was obtained from:
J.T. Batchelor Ltd. Leather Merchants
9–10 Culford Mews
London N1 4DZ
Tel: +44 (0)20 7254 2962

String (or twine) comes in various
thicknesses and is not always labeled with
an exact amount, so you may need to
experiment with a single ball to start
with. The String Stool (pages 54–7) was
made with natural-coloured kitchen twine,
which is available from hardware and
stationery stores.

Metallic wire is available in a variety of
thicknesses in craft stores of from wire
merchants. The 24 gauge (0.5mm thick)
wire used for the Moulded Wire Mat (see
pages 86–9) was obtained from:
The Scientific Wire Company, 18 Raven
Road, London E18 1HW
Tel: +44 (0)20 8505 0002
www.wires.co.uk

Yarn suppliers

To obtain Rowan and Jaeger yarns, look below to find a distributor or store in your area. For the most up-to-date list of stores selling Rowan yarns, visit their website:

www.knitrowan.com

Selected Rowan and Jaeger stockists

AVON
Bath: Rowan at Stitch Shop,
15 The Podium, Northgate.
tel: +44 (0) 1225 481134
Bristol: Rowan at John Lewis,
Cribbs Causeway.
tel: +44 (0) 117 959 1100
Rowan at House of Fraser,
The Horsefair.
tel: +44 (0) 117 944 5566
Staple Hill: Knitting Well,
105 High Street.
tel: +44 (0) 117 970 1740

BEDFORDSHIRE
Leighton Buzzard: Rowan at Needle & Thread,
2/3 Peacock Mews.
tel: +44 (0) 1525 376456
Luton: Kaytes Needlecrafts,
4 The Gallery, Arndale Center.
tel: +44 (0) 1582 48251

BERKSHIRE
Reading: Rowan at John Lewis,
Broad Street.
tel: +44 (0) 1189 575955
Windsor: W. J. Daniels & Co Ltd,
120-125 Peascod Street.
tel: +44 (0) 1753 862106

BUCKINGHAMSHIRE
Milton Keynes: Rowan at John Lewis,
Central Milton Keynes.
tel: +44 (0) 1908 679171

CAMBRIDGESHIRE
Cambridge: Rowan at Robert Sayle,
St Andrews Street.
tel: +44 (0) 1223 361292

Peterborough: Rowan at John Lewis,
Queensgate Centre.
tel: +44 (0) 1733 344644

CHESHIRE
Cheadle: Rowan at John Lewis,
Wilmslow Road.
tel: +44 (0) 161 491 4914

CORNWALL
Penzance: Iriss,
66 Chapel Street.
tel: +44 (0) 1736 366568
www.iriss.co.uk
Truro: Rowan at Truro Fabrics,
105/106 Kenwyn Street.
tel: +44 (0) 1872 222130
www.trurofabrics.co.uk
Wadebridge: Rowan at Artycrafts,
41 Molesworth Street.
tel: +44 (0) 1208 812274

COUNTY DURHAM
Darlington: Rowan at Binns,
7 High Row.
tel: +44 (0) 1325 462606

CUMBRIA
Brampton: The Bobbin Box,
Unit 2, Old George Market Place.
tel: +44 (0) 1697 73611
Penrith: Rowan at Indigo,
1 St Andrews View.
tel: +44 (0) 1768 899917
www.indigoknits.co.uk
Just Sew, Poet Walk.
tel: +44 (0) 1768 866791

DEVON
Bideford: Wool and Needlecraft Shop,
49 Mill Street.
tel: +44 (0) 1237 473015
Exeter: Inspirations,
7 Piazza Terracina, Haven Road.
tel: +44 (0) 1392 435115
Plymouth: Rowan at Dingles,
40-46 Royal Parade.
tel: +44 (0) 1752 266611

Totnes: Sally Carr Designs,
The Yarn Shop,
31 High Street.
tel: +44 (0) 1803 863060

DORSET
Christchurch: Honora,
69 High Street.
tel: +44 (0) 1202 486000
www.knittingyarns.co.uk
Dorchester: Goulds Ltd,
22 South Street.
tel: +44 (0) 1305 217816
Sherbourne: Hunters of Sherborne,
4 Tilton Court,
Digby Road.
tel: +44 (0) 1935 817722
Swanage: The Wool & Craft Shop,
17 Station Road.
tel: +44 (0) 1929 422814
Wimbourne: Rowan at The Walnut Tree,
1 West Borough.
tel: +44 (0) 1202 840722

ESSEX
Chelmsford: Franklins,
219 Moulsham Street.
tel: +44 (0) 1245 346300
Colchester: Franklins,
13/15 St Botolphs Street.
tel: +44 (0) 1206 563955
Maldon: Peachey Ethknits,
6/7 Edwards Walk.
tel: +44 (0) 1621 857102
www.ethknits.co.uk
Southend-on-Sea: Gades,
239 Churchill South,
Victoria Circus.
tel: +44 (0) 1702 613789

GLOUCESTERSHIRE
Cheltenham: Rowan at Cavendish House,
The Promenade.
tel: +44 (0) 1242 521300
Cirencester: Ashley's Wool Specialist,
62 Dyer Street.
tel: +44 (0) 1285 653245

GREATER MANCHESTER

Didsbury: Rowan at Sew In of Didsbury,
741 Wilmslow Road.
tel: +44 (0) 161 4455861
www.knitting-and-needlework.co.uk
Marple: Rowan at Sew In of Marple,
46 Market Street.
tel: +44 (0) 161 427 2529
www.knitting-and-needlework.co.uk

HAMPSHIRE

Basingstoke: Pack Lane Wool Shop,
171 Pack Lane,
Kempshott.
tel: +44 (0) 1256 323644
Lymington: Leigh's,
56 High Street.
tel: +44 (0) 1590 673254
New Milton: Smith Bradbeer & Co Ltd,
126-134 Station Road.
tel: +44 (0) 1425 613333
Southampton: Rowan at John Lewis,
West Quay Shopping Centre.
tel: +44 (0) 238 021 6400
Winchester: C & H Fabrics,
8 High Street.
tel: +44 (0) 1962 843355

HERTFORDSHIRE

Boreham Wood: The Wool Shop,
29 Shenley Road.
tel: +44 (0) 20 8905 2499
Hemel Hempstead: Needlecraft,
142 Cotteralls.
tel: +44 (0) 1442 245383
St Albans: Alison's Wool Shop,
63 Hatfield Road.
tel: +44 (0) 1727 833738
Watford: Rowan at John Lewis,
The Harlequin, High Street.
tel: +44 (0) 1923 244266
Welwyn Garden City: Rowan at John Lewis.
tel: +44 (0) 1707 323456

ISLE OF MAN

Peel: Fabric Centre,
2 Crown Street.
tel: +44 (0) 1624 844991

KENT

Broadstairs: The Wool Box,
66 High Street.
tel: +44 (0) 1843 867673
Canterbury: Rowan at C & H Fabrics,
2 St George's Street.
tel: +44 (0) 1227 459760
Greenhithe: Rowan at John Lewis,
Bluewater.
tel: +44 (0) 1322 624123
Headcorn: Katie's Workbox,
15 High Street, Nr Ashford.
tel: +44 (0) 1622 891065
Maidstone: Rowan at C & H Fabrics,
68 Week Street.
tel: +44 (0) 1622 762060
Tunbridge Wells: Rowan at C & H Fabrics,
113/115 Mount Pleasant.
tel: +44 (0) 1892 522618

LANCASHIRE

Accrington: Rowan at Sheila's Wool Shop,
284 Union Road, Oswaldtwistle.
tel: +44 (0) 1254 875525
Barnoldswick: Rowan at Whichcrafts?,
29 Church Street.
tel: +44 (0) 1282 851003
www.whichcrafts.co.uk
Lytham: Rowan at Lytham Wools,
Unit 7, Market Hall, Market Square.
tel: +44 (0) 1253 732150
www.lythamwools.co.uk
Preston: Rowan at Bow Peep,
136 Liverpool Road, Longton.
tel: +44 (0) 1772 614508

LEICESTERSHIRE

Hinckley: Busy Fingers,
104 Castle Street.
tel: +44 (0) 1455 631033
Oakham: The Wool Centre,
17 The Market Place.
tel: +44 (0) 1572 771358

LINCOLNSHIRE

Lincoln: Binns,
226/231 High Street.
tel: +44 (0) 1522 524333

LONDON

Central: Rowan at Liberty,
Regent Street, W1.
tel: +44 (0) 20 7734 1234
Rowan at John Lewis,
Oxford Street, W1.
tel: +44 (0) 20 7629 7711
Rowan at Peter Jones,
Sloane Square, SW1.
tel: +44 (0) 20 7730 3434
Barnes: Creations,
79 Church Road, SW13.
tel: +44 (0) 20 8563 2970
Brent Cross: Rowan at John Lewis,
Brent Cross Shopping Centre, NW4.
tel: +44 (0) 20 8202 6535
Chiswick: Creations,
29 Turnham Green Terrace, W4.
tel: +44 (0) 20 8747 9697
Finsbury Park: Lenarow,
169 Blackstock Road.
tel: +44 (0) 20 7359 1274
www.lenarow.co.uk
Penge: Rowan at Maple Textiles,
188/190 Maple Road.
tel: +44 (0) 20 8778 8049
West Ealing: Bunty's at Daniels,
96/122 Uxbridge Road, W13.
tel: +44 (0) 20 8567 8729
www.bunty-wool.co.uk

MERSEYSIDE

Liverpool: Rowan at John Lewis,
Basnett Street.
tel: +44 (0) 151 709 7070
Prescot: Prescot Knitting Co Limited,
32 Eccleston Street.
tel: +44 (0) 151 426 5264
St Helens: The Knitting Centre,
9 Westfield Street.
tel: +44 (0) 1744 23993
Wallasey: Ryder House,
44 Seaview Road.
tel: +44 (0)151 691 1037

MIDDLESEX

Shepperton: Arts & Yarns,
Squires Garden Centre,

Halliford Road.
tel: +44 (0) 1932 781141

NORFOLK
East Dereham: Central Norfolk Knitting Machines,
4 Aldiss Court.
tel: +44 (0) 1362 694744
Norwich: Rowan at John Lewis,
All Saints Green.
tel: +44 (0) 1603 660021
Sheringham: Creative Crafts,
47 Station Road.
tel: +44 (0) 1263 823153.
www.creative-crafts.co.uk

NORTHAMPTONSHIRE
Holdenby: Patchwork Palace,
The Stable Yard,
Holdenby Howe.
tel: +44 (0) 1604 771303
www.patchworkpalace.com

NOTTINGHAMSHIRE
Nottingham: Rowan at John Lewis,
Victoria Centre.
tel: +44 (0) 115 9418282

OXFORDSHIRE
Burford: Burford Needlecraft Shop,
117 High Street.
tel: +44 (0) 1993 822136
www.needlework.co.uk
Oxford: Rowan at Rowan,
102 Gloucester Green.
tel: +44 (0) 1865 793366

SOMERSET
Taunton: Hayes Wools,
150 East Reach.
tel: +44 (0) 1823 284768
Yeovil: Enid's Wool & Craft Shop,
Church Street.
tel: +44 (0) 1935 412421

STAFFORDSHIRE
Stafford: Amerton Farm,
Stowe by Chartley.
tel: +44 (0) 1889 270294
www.amertonfarm.com
Wolstanton: K2 Tog,
111 High Street.
tel: +44 (0) 1782 862332.

SUFFOLK
Bury St Edmunds: Rowan at Jaycraft,
78 St John's Street.
tel: +44 (0) 1284 752982

SURREY
Banstead: Maxime Wool & Craft Shop,
155 High Street.
tel: +44 (0) 1737 352798
Camberley: Army & Navy,
45-51 Park Street.
tel: +44 (0) 1276 63333
Guildford: Pandora,
196 High Street.
tel: +44 (0) 1483 572558
Kingston-upon-Thames: Rowan at John Lewis,
Wood Street.
tel: +44 (0) 20 8547 3000

SUSSEX – EAST
Battle: Battle Wool Shop,
2 Mount Street.
tel: +44 (0) 1424 775073
Brighton: Rowan at C & H Fabrics,
179 Western Road.
tel: +44 (0) 1273 321959
Eastbourne: Rowan at C & H Fabrics,
82/86 Terminus Road.
tel: +44 (0) 1323 410503
East Hoathley: The Wool Loft,
Upstairs at Clara's,
9 High Street.
tel: +44 (0) 1825 840339
Forest Row: Village Crafts,
The Square.
tel: +44 (0) 1342 823238
www.village-crafts.co.uk
Lewes: Rowan at Kangaroo,
70 High Street.
tel: +44 (0) 1273 478554
www.kangaroo.uk.com

SUSSEX – WEST
Arundel: Rowan at David's Needle-Art,
37 Tarrant Street.
tel: +44 (0) 1903 882761
Chichester: Rowan at C & H Fabrics,
33/34 North Street.
tel: +44 (0) 1243 783300
Horsham: Rowan at The Fabric Shop,
62 Swan Walk.
tel: +44 (0) 1403 217945

Shoreham by Sea: Rowan at Shoreham Knitting,
19 East Street.
tel: +44 (0) 1273 461029
www.englishyarns.co.uk
Worthing: Rowan at The Fabric Shop,
55 Chapel Road.
tel: +44 (0) 1903 207389

TEESIDE
Hartlepool: Rowan at Bobby Davison,
101 Park Road.
tel: +44 (0) 1429 861300
www.woolsworldwide.com

TYNE AND WEAR
Newcastle-upon-Tyne: Rowan at John Lewis,
Eldon Square.
tel: +44 (0) 191 232 5000

WARWICKSHIRE
Warwick: Warwick Wools,
17 Market Place.
tel: +44 (0) 1926 492853

WEST MIDLANDS
Birmingham: Rowan at Beatties,
16-28 Corporation Street.
tel: +44 (0) 121 644 4000
Coventry: Busy Fingers,
29 City Arcade.
tel: +44 (0) 2476 559644
Solihull: Stitches,
355 Warwick Road,
Olton.
tel: +44 (0) 121 706 1048
Rowan at John Lewis,
Touchwood.
tel: +44 (0) 121 704 1121
Wolverhampton: Rowan at Beatties,
71-78 Victoria Street.
tel: +44 (0) 1902 422311

WILTSHIRE
Calne: Handi Wools,
3 Oxford Road.
tel: +44 (0) 1249 812081

WORCESTERSHIRE
Kidderminster: Woolwise,
10 Lower Mill Street.
tel: +44 (0) 1562 820279

NORTH YORKSHIRE
Nr Skipton: Rowan at Embsay Crafts,
Embsay Mills,
Embsay.
tel: +44 (0) 1756 700946
www.embsaycrafts.com
Whitby: Rowan at Bobbins,
Wesley Hall,
Church Street.
tel: +44 (0) 1947 600585
www.bobbins.co.uk
York: Rowan at Craft Basics,
9 Gillygate.
tel: +44 (0) 1904 652840

SOUTH YORKSHIRE
Barnsley: Knit Wits,
11 Church Street,
Royston.
tel: +44 (0) 1226 725527
Sheffield: Rowan at John Lewis,
Barkers Pool.
tel: +44 (0) 114 2768511

WEST YORKSHIRE
Castleford: Bromley & Vairy,
5 Vickers Street.
tel: +44 (0) 1977 603069
Hebden Bridge: Rowan at Attica,
2 Commercial Street.
tel: +44 (0) 1422 844327
www.attica-yarns.co.uk
Holmfirth: Rowan at Up Country,
78 Huddersfield Road.
tel: +44 (0) 1484 687803
www.upcountry.co.uk
Leeds: The Wool Shop,
Whingate Junction, Tong Road.
tel: +44 (0) 113 263 8383

THE WIRRAL
Brimstage: Rowan at Voirrey Embroidery Centre,
Brimstage Hall.
tel: +44 (0) 151 342 3514

WALES
Aberystwyth: Clare's,
13 Great Darkgate Street.
tel: +44 (0) 1970 617786
Cardiff: Rowan at David Morgan Ltd,
26 The Hayes.
tel: +44 (0) 29 2022 1011

Conway: Ar-y-Gweill,
8 Heol Yr Orsaf,
Llanrwst.
tel: +44 (0) 1492 641149
Fishguard: Jane's of Fishguard,
14 High Street.
tel: +44 (0) 1348 874443
Penarth: Rowan at David Morgan Ltd,
20 Windsor Road.
tel: +44 (0) 29 2070 4193
Swansea: Rowan at Mrs Mac's,
2 Woodville Road,
Mumbles.
tel: +44 (0) 1792 369820
Whitland: Rowan at Colourway,
Market Street.
tel: +44 (0) 1994 241333
www.colourway.co.uk

SCOTLAND
Aberdeen: Rowan at John Lewis,
George Street.
tel: +44 (0) 1224 625000.
Alford: Rowan at The Wool Shed,
Alford Heritage Centre,
Mart Road.
tel: +44 (0) 1975 562906
Berwickshire: Rowan at Moondance Wools,
Springhill Farm,
Coldingham,
Eyemouth.
tel/fax: +44 (0) 18907 71541
Edinburgh: Rowan at John Lewis,
St James Centre.
tel: +44 (0) 131 556 9121
Rowan at Jenners,
48 Princes Street.
tel: +44 (0) 131 225 2442
Glasgow: Rowan at John Lewis,
Buchanan Galleries.
tel: +44 (0) 141 353 6677
Isle of Arran: Trareoch Craft Shop,
Balmichael Visitors Centre,
Shiskine.
tel: +44 (0) 1770 860515
Kilmalcolm: Strathclyde Threads,
3 Drumpellier Place.
tel: +44 (0) 1505 873841
Lanark: Strands,
8 Bloomgate.
tel: +44 (0) 1555 665757

Linlithgow: Nifty Needles,
56 High Street.
tel: +44 (0) 1506 670435
St Andrews: Rowan at Di Gilpin
@ The Wool Merchants,
Burghers Closer,
141 South Street.
tel: +44 (0) 1334 476193
www.handknitwear.com
Stirling: Rowan at McAree Bros Ltd,
55-59 King Street.
tel: +44 (0) 1786 465646
www.mcadirect.com

Acknowledgements

My sincerest and most heart-felt thanks and appreciation to the hugely professional and extraordinarily creative collection of people who have put this book together. The truly empathetic team at Quadrille Publishing: my mentor Jane O'Shea for her unswerving belief and encouragement, my rock, editor Lisa Pendreigh, for her discernment, expertise, support and innate patience. The exceptional Helen Lewis and Ros Holder for inherent style and sublime design. The wonderful Graham Atkins Hughes who certainly helps to make craft sexy via his exquisite and inspirational photography. And Raol, of course. Sally Lee for her tireless enthusiasm and creativity, amazing spirit and friendship – this really wouldn't have happened without you! Pauline Turner for her invaluable professionalism, the hugely creative Hilary Jagger – thank you for getting involved – and my unique Hannah Davis. Also to Margaret Callaghan, who has the best vintage textile emporium in the country at 30a Upper St James Street, Brighton. Stephen Sheard of Coats Craft UK for always championing me and Kate Buller and her amazing team at Rowan Yarns for their incalculable and constant support. Tony Brooks at Yeoman Yarns for his invaluable sponsorship. Finally, Dolores York and her team at Reader's Digest for their belief in this project.